CIVIL SURVIVAL

Legal Guide

Civil Survival Series

Your Rights in Divorce
and Child Custody

Amanda DuBois

Our goal at Civil Survival is to get the information in these books out to all of the people who need it. Please visit our Web site to learn about large quantity distribution or to order single books. You are also welcome to call us at 206-547-9688 or email us at info@CivilSurvival.com for more information.

Books in the Civil Survival Series

Your Rights at Work Legal Guide
Your Rights at Work Workbook

Your Rights in Divorce and Child Custody Legal Guide
Your Rights in Divorce and Child Custody Workbook

Your Rights Renting a Home Legal Guide
Your Rights Renting a Home Workbook

Your Rights in the Criminal Justice System Legal Guide
Your Rights in the Criminal Justice System Workbook

Your Rights in an Accident Legal Guide
Your Rights in an Accident Workbook

Online Learning and Educational Products

www.LawClass.net
www.CivilSurvival.com

Thanks to my clients who showed me what was missing in our legal system. And thanks so much to Philip, Julia, and Madeleine, who supported me in fulfilling the promise of this book series. — A.D.

Published by
Civil Survival LLC,
927 N. Northlake Way, #210
Seattle, WA 98103
(206) 547-9688
www.CivilSurvival.com

FIRST EDITION
Illustrations by William E.G. Johnson
Book Design by Shannon McCafferty Design

Library of Congress Cataloging-in-Publication Data
Amanda DuBois.
Civil Survival Series: Your Rights in Divorce and Child Custody.

13-digit ISBN 978-0-9793936-8-6

1. Legal Reference 2. General Interest 3. Educational Series
I. Title: Civil Survival Series: Your Rights in Divorce and Child
          Custody. II. Series

This publication is intended as a general educational review of a legal subject. It is not intended as a source of advice for the solution of legal matters or problems. This publication is provided with the understanding that the authors and publisher are not giving legal advice or services. For advice on legal matters, the reader should consult an attorney.

Contents

Introduction 1

A Cautionary Tale: Our Case Study 5

1 • Marriage, Then and Now....................................... 22

2 • Marriage: What It Means for
    Property and Debts.. 28

3 • Divorce: Different in Different States...................... 37

4 • Fair and Equitable Distribution
    of Assets and Debts 43

5 • Who Gets the Kids? Custody Questions 51

6 • Child Support 72

7 • Alimony or Maintenance 79

8 • The Practical Side of the Divorce Process:
    How It All Comes Together 85

9 • Domestic Violence... 99

10 • Living Together but Not Married?
    Nonmarital Relationships 106

11 • Details, Details: It Doesn't End
    at the Courthouse 112

12 • Other Issues.. 116

Summary of Statutes.. 120

Six Things to Consider If You Think
    Your Marriage Is Ending 121

Glossary... 124

Resources.. 131

Index... 134

Introduction

The United States Declaration of Independence asserts that all people "are created equal . . . with certain unalienable Rights." Among these, it states, are "Life, Liberty, and the pursuit of Happiness." The Constitution promises these rights to every citizen. But how can we, as U.S. citizens, fulfill this promise for ourselves if we don't know the rules of the game? The *Civil Survival Series* is designed to make it easier for everyone to understand these very important rules. We know that our legal system is the foundation on which our society is built. Therefore, in order to succeed in life, we must have some understanding of basic legal concepts. We won't learn it all in a day or a week—understanding U.S. law involves a lot of exploring—but the *Civil Survival Series* is a very good place to start.

Civil Survival cannot take the place of a lawyer, however. The series does not offer specific legal advice. Rather, *Civil Survival* is simply an educational tool intended to teach basic, general legal principles. Every real-life situation is different, and every city, county, and state has many laws that could affect your legal rights. **Please do not rely on *Civil Survival* for real-life legal problems.**

If you believe you need legal advice, there are many resources available. You can contact a lawyer or a local legal clinic. There is no guarantee that the content in this *Your Rights in Divorce and Child Custody: Legal Guide* is up to date or accurate enough to be relied on instead of a lawyer. Please remember that the *Civil Survival Series* is not a substitute for the advice of a trained lawyer.

Chances are good that you already know something about many of the topics discussed in this *Your Rights in Divorce and Child Custody: Legal Guide*. Most of us are in some kind of relationship, with a spouse, a boyfriend or girlfriend, or a partner. Many of these relationships are happy, but some of them end in a breakup or divorce. And the kids! The kids in a marriage or a relationship make life wonderful and complicated at the same time. This legal guide deals with all those topics—marriage, divorce, child custody, and other family-related matters. But there's a lot more too. You'll learn general principles about property laws and about how divorce courts usually divide the assets from a marriage or a long-term relationship. You'll see that although the principles are generally the same, every state has its own views on divorce, child custody, alimony, and child support. So you can see why it's important to become familiar with your state's laws about divorce.

In the *Your Rights in Divorce and Child Custody: Legal Guide*, many questions ask you to talk to other people about the experiences they've had. You'll learn about how you are able to find information about the laws in your state. Many useful Web sites are highlighted throughout this guide. You'll find organizations and agencies that can help with a variety of problems that deal with marriage and family law. You'll notice one thing right away: Even though this guide is divided into chapters, the topics seem to fit together like a jigsaw puzzle. That's the way it is when the legal system has to sort out the problems that go along with divorce. The questions of financial support and child custody, for example, can't be entirely separated.

And here's one big warning: This information is *not* put together so you can find all the things that might be wrong in your marriage or relationship. It's *not* a checklist of complaints. Instead, the *Your Rights in Divorce and Child Custody: Legal Guide* is designed to help you plan ahead. This way you can protect yourself, your children, and your rights, both during a long relationship and afterward, if it has to end. You can also learn more online, by going to the *Your Rights in Divorce and Child Custody: E-Learning Studio* on the Web at www.CivilSurvival.com. In the *E-Learning Studio* activities there are lots of examples of how the law might apply in certain situations. The activities also show how complicated it can get when different laws affect specific situations.

At the end of this guide are three important sections. One is the glossary. It's a list of the terms used throughout the book, so you can look something up if it doesn't make sense. You will also find a list of resources in the back that includes all the major books, Web sites, and other references used throughout the guide. Finally, the index is alphabetical, like the glossary. It tells you where different topics can be found in the *Your Rights in Divorce and Child Custody: Legal Guide.* So if you want to look at a particular legal concept or example again, you can find it easily by looking in the index.

The *Your Rights in Divorce and Child Custody: Legal Guide* also includes icons. You can use these tools to help find information faster and easier. Look through this list, and you'll see how helpful they can be.

Resources—Look here to find out more, like URLs (Web site addresses), books, and other references.

Take Note—These are helpful hints and suggestions pointing out what you can do.

Key Points—Terms, important concepts, and central topics are highlighted this way.

Statutes—Names and descriptions of laws and legal codes.

Are you ready for an adventure in *Civil Survival?* Great! Let's jump right into *Your Rights in Divorce and Child Custody*. Remember, you can always visit us online at www.CivilSurvival.com.

A Cautionary Tale:
Our Case Study

Breanna turned up the music on her stereo as high as it would go—anything to block out the escalating argument between her parents in the kitchen directly below her bedroom. She never thought putting the bread in the bread drawer upside down could be cause for such a fight, but over the past several months her parents had complained about nearly anything and everything.

"Breanna?" The voice was as small as the gap-toothed six-year-old who stood in her big sister's doorway.

Breanna forced a smile. "C'mon in, Han." Hana ran open-armed across the room and crashed into her sister's bed. She clutched her stuffed alligator under her arm. "Let's watch some TV," suggested Breanna. She grabbed the remote and scanned past Jay Leno to Nickelodeon, where SpongeBob Squarepants and his friend Patrick were desperately trying to get out of Bikini Bottom. Breanna hit the volume button in hopes of drowning out the chaos downstairs.

Before long, the television and Breanna's down comforter had done their jobs, providing the girls with a strongly needed shelter.

Then *crash!* Their mother had probably thrown another wine glass at their father. Hana couldn't hold it in any longer. A gentle sob escaped from her quivering lips.

"Get out!" Their mother shouted at their father. Her voice was so shrill it was barely recognizable.

The girls' brother, Gavin, didn't bother to knock. Head down, he stoically picked his way across the floor strewn with his teenage sister's stuff and plopped himself on the end of the bed.

Breanna threw back the comforter and Gavin climbed in, his back to his sisters.

"Out!" their mother screamed again.

A door slammed and the house rumbled with the familiar screeching of the ancient garage door. The kids looked at each other in silence as their father's old Subaru wagon powered down the dark street.

The Children's Best Interests

Insook Reilly was nervous about this appointment. And it had been hard to leave the hair salon she owned even for an hour. But she knew she needed to get some information about getting a divorce.

She looked across the desk at the tall woman in the stylish black suit. "He says he wants the house and the children," Insook began.

"Well, we can start by talking about your family. How many kids do you have?" The attorney, Robin Rosenberg, could see that this would be a painful experience for her new client.

Insook rummaged around in her purse and pulled out a picture of Breanna, Gavin, and Hana. They were standing with the family's mixed-breed mutt in front of the trailer parked next to the river on their vacation property. "Three. These past few months have been really hard on them."

"They're darling." The lawyer took off her glasses. "Tell me a little bit about how you and your husband divide up the child-care duties."

The tissue in Insook's hand had nearly disintegrated, but she scrunched it up anyway and tried to use it to wipe away the mascara that was streaking down her cheeks. "What do you mean?"

The lawyer held out the rapidly dwindling supply of tissue in a pretty red box. "Who's primarily responsible for the day-to-day care of the children?"

Insook shrugged. "Gee, I don't know. Andy drives the morning carpool, and I try to pick the kids up at their after-school activities and spend a few hours with them before I go back to work each evening."

"Who gets them up and ready for school?"

"Andy does the morning stuff. I get them home after school and spend an hour at home with them. Then I need to get back to one or another of the hair salons I own. Andy takes care of dinnertime, but usually I'm home in time to eat with the kids."

"So Andy fixes the meals?"

"Well, yes, but he's got more free time than I do." Insook realized she sounded guilty, like she was making excuses about not spending more time with her kids.

The lawyer scribbled notes as they spoke. "Homework?"

"What about it?" asked Insook.

"Who helps with homework?"

"I guess we both do that. I have a good head for numbers, so I help them with math. Andy's better at the other stuff, you know, history and social studies."

"I take it you both go to parent-teacher conferences and other school activities?"

"I try, but my job is pretty demanding, so sometimes I have to miss school events."

The lawyer sighed. "Do either of you volunteer in the classroom?"

"Andy works for his own landscaping company, and he doesn't work long hours. So he's able to go with the kids on some of their field trips." Insook paused. "Why are you asking me all this? What difference does it make? I love those kids every bit as much as he does."

Robin nodded in sympathy and smiled to let Insook know she wasn't criticizing her. Then she explained why she had asked all those questions. "Child custody is determined by what is called the 'children's best interest.'"

"Well, the children's best interest is to be with *me*. I'm their mother!"

"I know it seems that way, but the law in this state directs the judge to look to see which parent has fulfilled the majority of the parenting functions over the past year or so. The goal is for the court to try and maintain the status quo—which means they try to keep things as much as possible they were before the breakup. That way the children's lives are upset as little as possible."

"Are you telling me that Andy may actually be able to get custody?" Insook's voice shook, and her tears were about to start up again.

"It's certainly possible. It sounds like you and he split the parenting functions about equally. In fact, it sounds like he may have done more parenting than you have over the past year." Robin knew she had to be honest with Insook about the possibilities.

Insook buried her face in her hands; suddenly the mascara didn't seem all that important.

Robin waited a couple of minutes, then gently suggested, "Don't get discouraged. We'll work on that. But for now, tell me about your work and your family income. We have a lot to cover."

Insook explained how she had started her salon career by cutting hair right after she had finished high school. She had worked hard, and by the time she and Andy got married, she was on the way to buying a hair salon herself. By now, after eleven years of marriage, she owned three salons around town and they were all very successful.

"What kind of income does your husband have?" the attorney asked.

"Um, he does okay. He doesn't work nearly as many hours as I do, though. He likes to take it easy. He's always complaining that I work too much, and I think he doesn't work enough." Insook sighed.

After a few more questions, Robin asked Insook if she understood the idea of "shared money." Insook shook her head—that was a new one to her.

"In this state, the courts divide marital property equitably. That means they look at everything you have earned or purchased during your marriage and divide it in a way that the court believes will be fair. If you divorce, it's likely that your husband will be entitled to half the value of your hair salons. That doesn't mean he gets half the salon; let's say the value of the salons is about the same as the value of your house, so he might get the house and you might get the salons. And we can definitely argue that he has no interest in the salon you had before you got married, but the other side will say that the increase in value is an asset of the community. You can see how this gets pretty messy."

Robin stopped and waited. This was a hard thing for many people to accept when hearing this information for the first time. "And if there are any retirement accounts, in this state those will be divided too."

Insook's face got red. "But I'm the one who put in all the work, all the long hours, dealt with all the problems with employees—do you mean to tell me that Andy could still take that *and* my retirement?" She glared at Robin, but the attorney was used to clients getting upset. Divorce was never easy.

Inherited Property

"Let's go over your other assets." Robin turned to a clean sheet of paper. "I assume you own your home?"

Insook sniffled as she tried to compose herself. She nodded.

"Do you have any other major assets?"

"Not besides the hair salons, but they're worth a lot."

Robin asked, "Did either of you bring any property into the marriage?"

"No, we married in our early twenties," Insook answered. "I had just the one shop when we got married. Well, I was paying to buy the shop."

"Have either of you inherited anything during your marriage?"

"Yeah, Andy's dad left him some vacation property."

"Did you say Andy owns his own landscaping

business?" Insook nodded as she blew her nose. "Would you characterize him as successful?"

"Not really, he doesn't really work full time, so he doesn't make all that much money. Even if he did, the work is seasonal."

"Did you two mutually agree to him working part time?"

Insook shrugged. "I guess so. We didn't have a plan, exactly. But we agreed that someone had to be more available to the kids, and since the salons take so much time, it seemed obvious that Andy should back off on his hours a bit."

"So, you make more than he does?" Robin asked.

"About three times as much." Insook forced a weak smile.

Marriage Counseling

The lawyer flipped thorough her notes and cocked her head. "Have you guys considered marriage counseling?"

Insook looked at the lawyer suspiciously. "Why do you ask?"

"I'm looking at your custody situation. Under the 'best interest of the children' test, it's not entirely clear which of you would be designated the primary parent, although Andy has a fairly good chance of being awarded primary-parent status. And with regard to the financial case, you may well have to give up more than 50 percent of your assets and end up paying maintenance, or alimony, to Andy."

"What?" Insook nearly shrieked.

"The questions of finances are tough, I know." Robin

continued, "But the parenting and custody problem is hard to deal with too." She paused. "Still, the most important thing is, you really owe it to your kids to try to avoid putting them through the agony of a divorce. It sounds like they need you, and with your current parenting arrangement, you may become a weekend parent while Andy becomes the primary parent, and I'm guessing that would be a disaster for you."

Insook slumped in her chair. "I don't know. We argue about almost everything. It seems like our marriage is too far gone to salvage. Sometimes I think it would be easier on the kids if one of us moved out, but it never occurred to me that Andy could be considered the primary parent. He's *not*, you know!"

Robin looked straight at Insook. "I strongly encourage you to give it a try. Go to a good marriage counselor and see if you can get back on track."

"You're right," Insook agreed. "We should give it one last shot."

The lawyer turned to her computer and wrote down some names from her contact list. "Here are a few good counselors. Why don't you give them a call? If you and Andy can't work things out, call me and I'll try to help you negotiate an amicable settlement and a parenting plan—it's called the 'child custody plan' in some states—that works for both of you."

"Do you think we could get a fifty-fifty custody split?"

"Maybe, but most child experts recommend that the children have one primary residence with the other parent having generous time with the children."

"But I can't live without my kids." Insook's words were

choked.

"But this is about your *kids'* needs, not yours," Robin answered softly.

Options to Complete the Divorce

"What if Andy doesn't agree to an amicable settlement?" Insook asked.

Robin explained, "We may have to file a motion in court for a temporary parenting plan and to decide who stays in the house until a judge ultimately decides who gets the children and who gets which assets, as well as alimony."

"Can it really get that bad?"

"It can get worse than bad. Most family law matters are decided on a motions calendar in family court." The lawyer tapped her pen on the desk. "In our county, court commissioners hear around ten cases each morning and afternoon. In other counties the motions may be heard by a judge. Either way, they can have as little as twenty minutes to hear arguments and make a decision that you have to live with until your trial."

"A trial?" Insook couldn't imagine herself in a court-room, talking about her failed marriage. It was just too painful.

"If you can't reach an acceptable settlement with your husband, you will have to go to trial. That's not a good situation. I can't emphasize enough how little time judges have to consider the cases they hear."

Insook grimaced at the thought of an overworked judge making decisions that would dramatically affect every aspect of her family members' lives. She wondered what qualified a person in a black robe to make these life-altering decisions. What would some strange judge know about her family? Would the judge really care that Breanna had just made the debate team? And that Gavin hit a grand slam home run in the Little League finals just last week? Would a judge sit in the waiting room at the hospital while Hana had tubes put in her ears?

There was no way that Insook could allow some judge to give orders about exactly how they would live their lives. But from what Robin was telling her, Insook knew she probably wouldn't have any control over what was about to happen.

Andy Meets a Different Kind of Attorney

The woman didn't wear a drop of makeup, and her stringy hair was drawn back in a plain rubber band like the one Andy Reilly had taken from the morning paper. Andy shook hands with the lawyer, who had a reputation for winning at all costs. His coworker had insisted that Andy hire only the best, most aggressive lawyer in town. Then he gave Andy the phone number for this attorney, Cindy Willcox.

"Sit." The lawyer pointed at the straight-backed chair alongside the banged-up conference room table. She made no effort at direct eye contact, which surprised Andy. She quickly turned her attention to the yellow legal pad in front of her.

"Assets?"

Andy shifted in his chair. "I beg your pardon?" He wondered if he had made the right choice by choosing this blunt and unfriendly lawyer.

The lawyer shoved a stray piece of hair back with a bobby pin. "I need to know what assets you have."

Andy cleared his throat. "We, uh, we have a house, uh, and a trailer on a vacation lot."

"What about stock, retirement accounts, that kind of thing?"

"I think Insook has some kind of 401(k)."

"Kids?"

"What about them?"

The lawyer sighed heavily. "How many?"

"Three: two girls and a boy. Breanna is—" but he didn't get a chance to finish, because Cindy cut him off.

"Who's the primary parent?"

"The what?"

"Which one of you makes breakfast, volunteers at school, takes the kids to the doctor, that kind of thing?"

"We both do."

The lawyer stopped and actually looked at Andy. She leaned forward. "Are you telling me that you participate in child rearing as much as your wife does?"

Andy looked around the cluttered conference room. "I . . . I guess so. I get the kids ready in the mornings and drive the carpool. Whenever she has time, my wife picks them up after their activities. She owns some hair salons, so she goes to work early. She tries to be home for an hour or so in the afternoon so she can see them after school. I generally make dinner and get the kids to bed while she works."

"The wife's a business owner?" A smirk swept across the lawyer's plain face. "We'll kick her butt!" Cindy nodded her head and chuckled.

Aggressive Tactics

Andy leaned forward. "What do you mean?" The attorney seemed to revel at the idea of an anticipated battle.

"I take it she makes more money than you do."

Andy nodded. He didn't want to tell this woman much about his own income. He had the feeling she might actually laugh at him.

"And you're a regular mister-mom kinda guy, right?" She winked at Andy. Why did it seem like this lawyer was making a joke?

"I certainly do my fair share of parenting." His parenting prowess felt somehow hollow as he watched the woman's eyes narrow into little slits. She didn't give a rip about his parenting abilities. And she clearly had no interest in his kids; she didn't even ask their names.

"So we'll get you 60 percent of the assets and full custody of the kids." The lawyer picked up the phone and summoned her assistant. Then she looked briefly at Andy. "Rebecca will take down your information so we have what we need for our motion for a temporary parenting plan and maintenance. You can expect a draft via fax within the week, and we'll be in court within the month."

Then Cindy Willcox headed for the door.

A Temporary Parenting Plan

"Excuse me." Andy spoke to the lawyer's back. "What's a 'temporary parenting plan'?"

"It's when I go to court to get your wife kicked out of the house and have you designated as the primary parent," she spoke over her shoulder. "We'll ask for maintenance and child support. I'll need sworn affidavits from your friends and the kids' teachers stating that you fulfill most of the parenting functions." The woman's voice had the abrupt monotone of a computerized voice.

Andy felt like he was on a telephone and had just been put on hold. And he still didn't see why they needed any kind of parenting plan. The problem was between him and Insook, not with their kids or their parenting.

Expensive Options

"How much is all this going to cost?" Andy had been warned by another friend about the high cost of lawyers' fees. His friend had said it was easy to let the lawyers eat up your hard-earned savings before you realized what had happened.

"Not much," the lawyer answered, her hand on the doorknob. "Less than five thousand," she said without missing a beat.

"Five thousand dollars?" Andy was shocked.

"For the first motion, where we kick her out."

"I'd like a couple of days to think about this." Andy was getting both nervous and angry.

Cindy crossed her arms and cocked her head. "And let your wife beat you to the courthouse?" She frowned. "I strongly recommend that you get yourself in the driver's seat on this one. You have a pretty good shot at getting the kids, and a good portion of your wife's business as well, but you have to act fast." The door slammed behind her.

Andy watched uneasily through the windows of the conference room as the lawyer steamrolled down the narrow hallway lined with legal books. Maybe she was right; maybe Insook would beat him to the courthouse and get the kids.

There had to be a better way to resolve this mess, he thought. He put his head in his hands and sat there, alone.

If the Parties Don't Get Along, the Court Decides

On the advice of Insook's lawyer, the couple decided to seek marriage counseling before beginning divorce proceedings. The marriage counselor had suggested that both Insook and Andy sign up for separate divorce-support groups. Insook's group met in the basement of the Congregational church. The coffee smelled days old and the cookies tasted stale, but they were nothing compared with the depressing discussion that followed among the women.

"My ex sent the kids home with a suitcase of dirty laundry again." The slightly overweight woman sitting next to Insook clenched her jaw.

"Nancy, you have to do something!" said the tall woman with frosted hair. "When my ex tries to pull off that kind of stuff, I drag his butt into court and get him fined for contempt."

"But he'll respond by accusing me of not shouldering my share of the kids' clothing allowance and activities," said Nancy.

A chill went up Insook's spine as the discouraged woman reached into her battered purse and pulled out a crinkled-up e-mail. Insook prayed that this wouldn't be her in a couple of years.

"Here's the list he sent me. He spent $458 on back-to-school stuff for our daughters and now he wants me to come up with my 35 percent."

Insook looked over the woman's shoulder to see a detailed list of everything from jeans and jackets down to hair clips and bracelets. "Why 35 percent?" she asked.

"We pay everything in proportion to our income, but he makes so much more than I do that I can never keep up." The woman crumpled up the list and threw it forcefully onto the floor in the middle of the circle.

Somehow Insook wasn't able to join in as the group members smiled and shook their heads. One shouted, "You go, girl!"

Then a pretty redhead spoke up. "I'd pay it if I were you. My ex took me to court last month for violating the court order about weekend visitation, and I ended up having to pay his attorney's fees. If it's in a court order, you gotta comply."

A knowing murmur swept through the musty basement room. Insook's heart ached for the women in the circle whose lives were ruled by overworked judges and family-court commissioners. It seemed that every dispute was decided with a bang of the gavel. She shuddered to think of the women's legal fees.

The overweight woman continued. "And that's not all; the jerk had my daughters tell me that he can't afford to keep them in the small private school they've been in since they were little. He didn't even have the decency to tell me himself." Her voice wavered. "No sirree, he just took them out to look at public schools." She shook a well-worn stapled bunch of legal papers. "The parenting plan clearly states that we're to make all decisions about education together! I'm sick of him deciding everything himself and then using the girls as his private messenger service."

"How do the girls feel about changing schools?" the redhead asked.

"They're devastated, but the selfish pig actually convinced them that if he had to keep paying tuition at Saint Anne's, he'd have to give up his football season tickets. Jennifer cried herself to sleep last night."

Insook blinked back the tears. She couldn't imagine putting her children in the middle of her differences with Andy. Right then, she vowed to put the children's needs ahead of her own. But what if he really did want to fight her for custody? What then?

The Kids React

Andy was worried. Breanna's grades had taken a nosedive since he and Insook had split up. She was quiet. He missed Breanna's bubbly laugh at the dinner table. But she kept a fierce eye on her little brother and sister, as if she were the only one who knew what they needed.

And Gavin, now ten, had started talking back. This was a new side to his son, and Andy didn't know how to handle it. He knew the coming divorce must have something to do with it though, and that made him feel guilty.

Most painful of all was the way little Hana suddenly seemed afraid. Many mornings she insisted she didn't feel good, and Andy was not willing to force her to go to school. After many absences, the school counselor finally called. By the end of that phone call, Andy knew that he needed to do something for his kids so they could survive the divorce too.

This was hard on everybody, and there seemed to be no end to the worries.

1 Marriage, Then and Now

I n the 1950s you can bet that almost no one had heard of a **parenting plan** or a custody arrangement. And back then, not many white men from middle- and upper-class backgrounds would have liked the idea that their wives might hold a job. (It is important to note, however, that women from economically disadvantaged backgrounds and many women of color have *always* worked outside the home.) And as for the kids? It's a whole new world these days for them.

But why a history lesson? It's interesting to look at some of the changes in marriage in the United States over the past hundred years or so. It might even be surprising to learn that not that long ago, women could not own property by themselves. Knowing about the past is helpful in understanding why the rules about marriage work the way they do today. A focus here on women's rights makes sense because it was the women who traditionally had the job of raising the children and managing the household. Some people would argue that women, by assuming these domestic duties, were primarily responsible for maintaining a safe and stable community and society.

Women's Roles in Colonial Times

When the earliest white European settlers came to North America, there wasn't much question about what rights women had. They basically had none. And things hadn't changed a lot by the time the colonies separated from England in the 1700s. Women did not own property. They didn't have the right to vote. Anything they owned before marriage became part of their husband's property when they married. Society expected all women to get married, because in the social structure they needed a man to support them.

What were women supposed to do, then? Have children and raise them and teach them. Lessons included reading and writing, but there was much more: instilling respect, patriotism, religious belief, and responsible behavior in the children. There was a lot to being a mother then, just as there is now.

By fulfilling these roles, women were supposed to help keep society running smoothly. They formed social groups that worked to improve the quality of life in their communities. They encouraged construction of schools and churches. One important example of how women tried to affect society was called the women's temperance movement. This was an attempt on the part of women to decrease the effect of alcohol abuse on society at large. "Temperance" is an old-fashioned word for self-control or self-restraint, and that's what many women's groups thought was missing in their communities. They felt that easy access to alcohol was harmful to a safe society, and eventually some states said alcohol could only be used for "medicinal purposes"—in other words, as medicine.

This led to a constitutional amendment in 1920 that made it against the law to buy or sell alcoholic beverages. This era in the United States was called Prohibition. The amendment was repealed in 1933.

Women's Property Rights Acts

In the 1800s, after the Civil War, things started to change for women. Many states passed laws that gave them some property rights; these were called the women's property rights acts. They were written to give women some rights in owning and keeping or inheriting property. Before these laws were enacted, any property a woman brought with her into marriage became the property of her husband, and she had no control over it. As a result of these property rights laws, if a woman owned property before she married, it remained her own property after she married. Her husband couldn't decide what to do with the property. He couldn't use it to pay his own debts, for example.

Now skip ahead to today. When a couple splits up, the judge would never automatically hand all the property to the man. Here's where you'll hear the term "**equitable distribution**" of property. (You'll learn all about this idea in chapter 5.) Part of the reason our courts try to distribute property this way is because of the women's property rights acts that were put in place more than a hundred years ago.

Another Big Issue: Suffrage

In 1919 a new amendment was added to the United States Constitution. The Nineteenth Amendment gave women an important new right: the right to vote. That's what

suffrage means—the right to vote. Here are the words of the amendment that make it clear:

STATUTE

> **The right of citizens of the United States to vote shall not be denied or abridged by the United States or by any State on account of sex.**

Okay, so what does this have to do with marriage? Let's use the example of the laws in most states that require the court to reach an equitable distribution of property in a divorce. Before women could vote, they had few property rights. After they began voting, however, the legislatures heard from women and added many laws making the divorce process more fair. So it can be said that the current laws regarding property began with women having the right to vote.

Another good example is the issue of domestic violence. First, remember that men can be victims of domestic violence too; it's not just women who get hit or abused. When laws were proposed that would punish someone who beat up his or her partner or spouse, one reason they got a lot of support was that women had the right to vote. The politicians changed the laws after they heard from enough women about abuse.

So How Important Is Marriage, Anyway?

Today, most women work outside the home. Sometimes they earn more than their husbands or partners do. Women own property, make investments, and write their own wills. In other words, they don't have to depend on men to live comfortably, if they don't want to. And on the flip side, men today are expected to take equal part in being good parents. They are expected to help with the kids and the household.

These days lots of couples live together before they marry. Other couples who live together don't ever marry. Gay and lesbian couples have children together. Some families think the mom should stay home with the kids. Other people have no problem with putting the kids in day care. Lots of different arrangements work—it just depends on the family. This book doesn't offer any easy answers about marriage and relationships. Each one of us has to decide for ourselves what kind of relationship we want. Then we have to figure out how to make that relationship work.

Still, this brings up interesting questions: How does American society view marriage and family relationships? Does our society value the family unit? Divorce is common, and lots of people suffer because of divorce. Does that mean society doesn't care about having stable families? Do our laws make it easier or harder for a family to stay together? Is it better for an unhappy family to stay together? As you can see, these are complicated questions.

 ## What Do You Think?

- Start noticing small details where you work or shop: Are more women or more men doing the grocery shopping these days? Who's waiting for the kids at the bus stop? Who takes the kids to the doctor or the library?

- Chances are good that you work with someone from another country. Maybe you yourself are from a country other than the United States. What's different about being a mom or a dad in this country, compared with what it's like to be a parent in other countries?

- Do you think today's laws about equitable distribution of property are fair to both men and women?

- Who do you think is better suited to raising kids alone, a mother or a father? Why?

- Talk to a senior citizen. Find out how he or she feels about the changes in American society that affect families. Here's a sample question: Do you think it's better to get a divorce or to stay in a marriage for the kids' sake?

- Do you think our society shows that the job of being a parent is highly valued? Why or why not?

2 Marriage: What It Means for Property and Debts

How many people think, before they get married, about whether or not they live in a **community-property state**? Should they sign a **prenuptial agreement** before they get married? What happens if one person owns an asset before the couple marries? Can that property become jointly owned property? What belongs to the husband and what belongs to the wife? What about the debt of one party? Does it matter if the debt existed before marriage, or whose name is on the debt? What exactly does it mean when you sign that marriage certificate? We'll explore all these questions in this chapter.

It's a Contract

A marriage is a **contract**. It doesn't matter what the exact words of your vows were. The vows don't describe the legal relationship between you and your spouse. Rather, the marriage relationship is defined by the state. In fact, the state laws about marriage and divorce are the terms of the contract. For example, the state defines

KEY POINT

which assets are separate and which are owned by the couple together. The best way to make sense of this is to look at what "separate" or "community property" means. But first let's define the word "asset."

What Exactly Is an Asset?

This is an important idea to understand. **Assets** are things that have value, like a house, a piece of property, a truck, or a boat. Savings accounts, stocks and bonds, and retirement accounts are also considered assets.

Then there's the idea of an **intangible asset**. "Intangible" means it's real but you can't touch it. One example of an intangible asset might be a law degree or a business. Can you spot the intangible assets in the case study? You're right—the salon businesses that Insook built from her early days as a hair stylist and Andy's landscaping business. Businesses have value if they're sold, but they could also have value for their ability to produce income. Those intangible assets are usually included in a divorce settlement, and that's one reason Andy's aggressive lawyer was excited when she heard Insook was a business owner.

As you know, part of the divorce process involves dividing assets. Whether you live in a marital property or community-property state, the court's job is to find a fair and equitable distribution of property. We'll take a closer look at property distribution in chapter 5, once we understand the legal concepts of **separate property** and marital property.

Separate Property

Separate property is recognized in most states, where it includes the assets owned by each spouse before marriage. It also usually includes gifts and inheritances even if they are received during the marriage. Separate property is treated differently from marital or community property in most states. So if you're thinking about getting a divorce, one of your first jobs is to identify which assets were owned before marriage as well as any gifts or inheritances you may have received during the marriage.

TAKE NOTE

Most of the time, separate assets are not divided in the divorce. However, if one spouse has a business that grows during the marriage, the business might be considered to be partly separate and partly marital, or community property. That's why Insook, in the case study, had good reason to be worried about her businesses.

Sometimes people mix their separate and marital assets. This is called "commingling." Keeping track of what you had when you got married may help you to untangle your commingled assets in the event of a divorce. Often, once the assets are commingled, it may be too late to make a separate property claim.

Now you can see why it's a good idea to take the necessary steps to protect the assets you bring into a marriage. Suppose your sister is getting married and her husband already owns a house. In most states, at the time of a divorce the house would still be considered the husband's separate property, even if your sister had paid part of the mortgage with her wages during the marriage. How can your sister protect herself so that (in the event of a divorce) she gets credit for using her hard-earned money to pay the mortgage payments on her new husband's house? She should ask a lawyer to help her protect herself under her state laws.

This is a good example of the importance of getting legal advice and possibly a prenuptial agreement before marriage. In the prenup the husband can state that the value of the house at the time of the marriage is his, but any value added after marriage would be considered marital property. However, if the husband does not agree to add his wife's name to the title on the house, it may be difficult in the event of a divorce for the wife to claim an interest in the house. Sometimes it's better if the original house is sold and the parties buy a new home in both their names. That way they both have an interest in the house (although the party who made the down payment may be able to get that back if there's a divorce).

It's important to get legal advice if you are planning to marry someone with assets, or if you have assets of your own that you want to protect. Don't commingle your separate assets by putting them in a joint account. Keep such assets in a separate account and don't add any assets to it once you marry. You can open a new account for your own use after you are married. The issue of separate property can be confusing, but the stakes are high, so you may want to consult a lawyer for a prenuptial agreement. Naturally, at the time of marriage no one expects to get a divorce, but it's better to be safe than sorry. We'll talk more about prenuptial agreements in chapter 13.

TAKE NOTE

Marital Property

Most states in our country use the concept of marital property. Property earned or accumulated during the marriage is considered marital property and is usually divided by the court during a divorce. This is true even if only one spouse's name appears on the title to the property. Common examples of marital property are homes, cars, or even bank or stock accounts. Marital property may also include businesses owned in whole or in part by one of the spouses. Most people are surprised to learn that many states consider retirement accounts to be marital property that can be divided in a divorce.

In the case study, for example, Insook owned one of the hair salons before she got married. However, at the time of divorce, the court will probably include her salons as an asset of the marriage, and that property would be included in the property distribution. The value of the salons may be reduced somewhat because part of the asset existed before marriage. Figuring this out often involves a financial expert such as a CPA (certified public accountant).

TAKE NOTE

You can see that divorces involving businesses can get complicated, so if you're thinking of divorce, it's a good idea to check with a lawyer, especially if either you or your spouse owns a business.

Community Property

There are nine community-property states: Arizona, California, Idaho, Louisiana, Nevada, New Mexico, Texas, Washington, and Wisconsin. Puerto Rico allows for community property too, and Alaska is an opt-in community-property state. In a community-property state each partner in a marriage owns one half of all of the assets that were purchased or earned during the marriage. If you bought a house, a car, or a vacation cabin during the marriage, that would all become community property. So is all money saved in retirement funds or pensions during the marriage. It doesn't matter whose income was used to purchase the asset, because in a community-property state even a person's wages are considered half owned by his or her spouse!

KEY POINT

The idea behind community property is that a marriage is like a partnership with two equal partners. Both partners contribute to the marriage, even if the contributions are not always financial. The court in community-property states does not try to figure out who bought what, or who did what for the other in the marriage. The court simply puts all of the assets earned or bought during the marriage into one big pot and divides it in two.

Community-property states also recognize the idea of separate property, and anyone living in a community-property state should remember to keep his or her separate property *separate* if that spouse wants to avoid having to divide that property with the other spouse upon divorce.

Let's look at the case study again. This time think of Insook and Andy as living in a community-property state. She earns a lot more than he does, but when they divorce, the assets they purchased during the marriage with their earnings are still considered community property. So even though Insook did all the work to grow her businesses, and she paid the majority of the bills (including the mortgage payment), in a community-property state Andy still owns half of all the assets, including the hair salons (less the value of the salon Insook owned before they got married). Andy also has a one-half interest in any money Insook put into her retirement fund during the marriage.

An Inheritance or Gift
Is Usually Treated Differently

In the case study, remember the picture of the kids in front of their vacation trailer? The lakefront property and the trailer were assets. That's right, the trailer is considered separate property because it was inherited, and in most states it probably would not be included as an asset to be divided in a divorce settlement.

The same is true of gifts. What if Andy's father had given him a CD (a certificate of deposit, which is an investment with a bank) worth $10,000? You're right again. That would be considered a gift and would probably not be included in a divorce settlement. However, if Andy cashed in the CD and put it into the family bank account, he could have difficulty showing that the $10,000 should be his separate property at the time of the divorce. What if Andy cashed in the CD and used the money to put a new roof on the family home? This is an example of when it would be necessary to hire an expert to try to "trace" the separate property.

When separate property gets mixed in with marital or community property, it is said to have been commingled and might be considered available for division in a divorce settlement. So remember to keep any monetary gifts you receive during marriage in a separate account and then

TAKE NOTE don't add anything to it!

Debts

It's not just a question of what you own—your assets—
when a marriage ends. There's also the unpleasant reality
of debts. Just like the courts divide assets, they also divide
debts in a divorce settlement. The biggest kinds of debt
besides a mortgage are car loans and credit card debt.

Debt generated before marriage is considered separate
debt. In addition, some states treat some types of debt
(most often credit card debt) as separate debt, depending
on which spouse signed the credit card application. Other
states consider all debt generated during marriage to be
joint debt. Any debt will be divided according to the law
of the state where you live, so it's important to understand how your state treats debt in a marriage.

TAKE NOTE

What Do You Think?

- List your significant assets. Could any of
  these assets be considered separate? Do you
  have any assets now that you owned before marriage?

- Now list your debts. Remember to include things like
  car loans or mortgages as well as credit card debt.
  How do you think your debts would be seen by a
  divorce court? Would any be considered separate?
  Check the law in your state to see if credit card debt
  is seen as the responsibility of the couple or the person whose name appears on the account.

- If you don't own intangible property (such as a business), talk to someone who does, and see how they
  would put a dollar value on it. Ask about the difference between the financial value and the emotional

value of the asset. Find out how he or she would feel about having a judge put a dollar value on the asset. How would this person feel about having to buy out his or her spouse for the half interest in the business? Do you think this is fair?

- How can you find out whether the state where you live is a community-property state? Would knowing that change anything about the way you handle your property? (Remember, property can include all sorts of things—from a car to a retirement account.)

- What kinds of records or documents would a person have to keep in order to show that he or she owned property before getting married? Why could this be important?

- Your best buddy is thinking about getting married, but you don't like his girlfriend. You think she's after his money. Can he protect the house he purchased before they even started dating?

- Here's a good one: The vows a couple says when they get married aren't the legally enforceable terms of the contract defined by the state that makes them a married couple. Try explaining to someone else the difference between marriage vows and a contract. It's the best way to see if you understand the difference yourself!

3 Divorce: Different in Different States

ne thing you need to know about divorce is that every state has different laws regarding the division of property and debts as well as the custody of children. In most states the legal principles are generally the same, but the way they're put into action may be different. For example, in some states divorces are considered to be "no fault," and other states require there to be a reason for the divorce. These reasons are called "**grounds for divorce**."

About one-third of the states in this country do not consider fault at all in the divorce process. These are called "no-fault states." Other states allow the parties to choose between fault and no-fault. Fault divorces usually take far longer and cost a lot more money than **no-fault divorces**. In some states there is a waiting period of separation before a court will enter a no-fault divorce. Only a handful of states have only fault divorces. Let's take a closer look at these legal concepts.

Grounds for Divorce

When you hear the phrase "**grounds for divorce**," it refers to the reasons for a state to grant a divorce. Some states

KEY POINT

don't accept the idea that a couple can just break up for no identified reason. The idea behind the requirement to show "grounds for divorce" is that divorce is hard on society and on families, so it shouldn't be allowed to happen easily. Those states require that the divorcing couple explain why they want a divorce. You'll read more about that below, when we talk about "fault" and "no-fault" divorces.

Not just any reason will do, either. For example, the State of New York doesn't currently accept **irreconcilable differences** as a reason to get divorced; "irreconcilable" means more or less the inability to get along with each other any more. What is considered a valid reason to divorce, then, in the New York courts? Some acceptable reasons include adultery, cruel and inhuman treatment, abandonment, and imprisonment. Even then there are conditions. You can divorce someone who has been in prison, but only if that person is confined for at least three years.

However, change is coming in New York, as lawmakers think about how to update divorce laws. Today, when a person files for divorce in New York, the party requesting the divorce must prove the reason for asking for the divorce. Recently there has been a movement in New York to add no-fault divorce to the existing divorce laws. The Web site of the New York State Bar Association (www.nysba.org) can give you good information about the rules in New York. Remember that a state legislature

RESOURCES can make changes in the laws at any time.

No-Fault States

Not everyone agrees with the idea that a couple should have to announce their reasons for divorcing. And since laws are written by the legislature for each individual state, the views of the people in a state can affect how those laws are shaped. So some states have developed laws that allow for no-fault divorces. A no-fault divorce means pretty much what it sounds like: the divorcing couple doesn't have to give a reason for why they're splitting up. They don't have to prove to a court or a judge that there is a problem in their marriage. In a no-fault divorce state the party asking for the divorce simply files for divorce and there is nothing the other spouse can do to stop the process. The state of Washington is an example of a no-fault state, and you can read more about its divorce rules at the Web site of the Washington State Bar Association (www.wsba.org).

RESOURCES

Using a good search engine on the Internet, you can easily find out whether the state where you live requires grounds for divorce or is a no-fault state. Type in "no-fault" or "grounds for divorce," then the name of the state.

Jurisdiction

One important thing to understand about the divorce process is that no matter which state you live in, once a divorce request is properly filed with the court, the court has the power to make decisions for the parties. Once a case is filed and the courts get this power, the court is said to have "**jurisdiction**" over the parties, their children, and their assets.

KEY POINT

So if the divorcing couple can't decide how to divide the assets, or they can't agree on a custody arrangement or child support, the court will decide for them. This is true even for temporary arrangements that arise during the period between the filing for divorce and the final settlement. For example, often the parties file a motion in court to have the court decide who will have custody of the children, or who will live in the house, or who will pay the bills on a temporary basis. This is discussed further in chapter 9.

Most people agree that it's better for people to try to make their own decisions about their assets and children, rather than the court. This is why it is very important for everyone thinking about a divorce to understand the principles of divorce and especially to understand their own state laws. If you understand these laws, you will be in a better position to decide on issues in your divorce, by following the principles that a court would likely follow. Of course, as always, it's a great idea to consult a lawyer or legal clinic that represents parties in family law issues in your state.

Sometimes a divorcing couple can divide their property and stay on friendly terms. Then there are couples who argue over every detail, down to **visitation rights** for the pets. The court then has to get involved in many details of the couple's lives. That's what people mean when they refer to an "ugly divorce." It's too bad that so much pain goes along with a breakup, because when it comes to divorce, there are certain steps the couple must go through, no matter how hurt or angry they are. The best way to handle this is to get the emotions under control, get support from family and friends, and then make a plan. You might want to consult with a lawyer in your area who practices family law. Do your homework and think about each step before you take it. That way you won't be as likely to have even bigger problems later. Remember, this guide is not meant to replace a trained lawyer; it is only here to educate you about some issues that may arise in a given situation.

You will notice that in the *Your Rights in Divorce and Child Custody: Legal Guide,* we often discuss what a court would do. This does not mean that most cases go to court; we mention the courts so you will know how to evaluate your own situation and hopefully come up with some ideas about a settlement for your case. The goal in most divorces is to avoid the expense and emotions of a court trial.

TAKE NOTE

What Do You Think?

• Explain to someone else the state's role in the marriage contract. (If you can't answer this now, don't worry—we'll talk more about it later.)

• This chapter talks about only a few of the ways courts have to get involved in a divorce. Talk to friends and family to learn what other ways a court ruling has affected them in a divorce or custody case.

• Your neighbor wants to make her ex "pay" for all the trouble she thinks he caused. Recall some details of her story and see if you can separate the facts from the emotions. Now imagine you are having the same discussion with the ex. Can you see his side of this issue? How would this issue be argued in a state where you must prove the reason for divorce? How about in a no-fault state?

- Find out if your state has fault divorce or no-fault divorce. Ask around to see what experiences friends or neighbors have had because of this.

- See if you can find at least one argument why it might be good to require grounds for divorce. Then see if you can find at least one good reason for why no-fault divorce might be better. Which of the two options seems more sensible to you? Why?

- Can someone go to court and ask a judge to make a ruling in a family law matter before a divorce case is filed? Why or why not? (Hint: Review the "Jurisdiction" section.)

4 Fair and Equitable Distribution of Assets and Debts

Most states have guidelines about deciding how assets are distributed. That means that most experienced lawyers will be able to tell a couple how the assets would most likely be divided if they were to go to court. So even though the parties might never get to court, the court has some influence in the divorce. And in the end, if the couple can't agree on a fair and equitable distribution of assets, the court will have to decide for them. That can get expensive fast.

Let's look again at the case study. Maybe Andy and In-sook tried marriage counseling, but nothing helped. They decided to divorce, but they couldn't agree on the terms. Even if their case did not end up in court, their lawyers would most likely negotiate a settlement or an agreement based on how a court would likely approach the case. In most states the court looks at many factors in order to decide how to divide up the property the couple had collected during their marriage.

Below is a short list of what factors are considered in most states when the court makes a decision about a fair and equitable distribution of assets. (The reason to understand this concept is so that you can begin to see how a case might be decided. Once you have this knowledge, you can better understand how to view your own situation.)

- How long the marriage lasted
- Any prenuptial agreements (legally binding agreements signed before the marriage)
- The age, health, and employability of each spouse
- The lifestyle the couple had during the marriage
- All sources of income for each spouse
- The future chances of each spouse to earn money or get more assets
- The economic circumstances or financial situation of each spouse when the property will be divided

KEY POINT

The court has the tough job of deciding what is equitable—what is most fair. So an equitable distribution is about trying to be fair, not about who did what to whom in the marriage, or why it ended. Property distribution in most states falls along fairly standard state guidelines. Basically, in most states the idea is to try to get close to a fifty-fifty division of assets. If the parties can't agree, the court steps in and determines the value of property, or determines whether or to what extent some assets are separate. Then the court comes up with what it believes is an equitable distribution. In some states, the larger share of the assets is given to the bigger wage earner. In some states, the larger share is given to the lower wage earner, with the thought that this person needs the additional head start.

Here are a few questions to consider when you think about the court's job in a divorce settlement: What if one spouse has job experience as a carpenter and is now in a wheelchair and can't work? How about a wife who always stayed home with the kids, and at the age of fifty-five she can't get a job that will pay the mortgage? What if one spouse can barely make ends meet working as a line cook, but the other spouse has a good union job with great health benefits and full retirement?

Let's look at another situation: A couple is used to a nice lifestyle. They have an RV and take nice long vacations every year. They have a cleaning service and a person who mows the lawn. If they divorce, what kind of lifestyle should each of them expect? Is it fair to ask one party to live on $2,000 a month when he or she was used to living on $6,000 a month? No wonder it's so complicated to figure out.

Other Considerations
When Dividing Property

It is important to understand the tax consequences of the division of property. Both parties must have a full understanding about which assets will have taxes associated with them if these assets are later sold. In cases such as these it's a good idea to meet with an accountant before agreeing to a property settlement.

Earlier in this guide you learned about different kinds of intangible assets, like a business or a high-paid career. Well, the courts have to have a way to value intangible assets. Below we discuss a couple of common situations faced by the courts. These are good examples of issues that often get decided by the court at trial because people can't agree on them in an out-of-court settlement.

Career Enhancement

The term "career enhancement" refers to how one spouse often makes choices or sacrifices in order to help the other spouse advance in his or her career. It's great as long as the marriage lasts, but those choices can have an impact on the terms of a divorce.

Think for a minute about a couple who moves around a lot for the husband's job. Maybe he's a foreman for a big construction company, or maybe he's in the military. His wife didn't have much chance to develop a career of her own because of the frequent moves, so she has little in the way of job experience and can't find a good job. In a divorce she can ask for consideration because of this, and it can come in a couple ways. She may ask for a larger portion of the assets (more than 50 percent). She might be entitled to **alimony** (also called "**maintenance**") until she can get some retraining and get back into the workforce. We'll talk more about alimony in a later chapter.

Business Ownership

Earlier we discussed business ownership as an example of an intangible asset. The first issue that must be figured out is the value of the business. Even a small auto shop or a nail salon has value. Most of the time, if the parties cannot agree on how to divide the assets when a business is involved, a CPA is hired to do what is called a "business valuation," which means that she or he inspects the financial statements of the business and determines its value.

There's another part to valuing a business. It's called "good will." That refers to the value a business has that can't be measured in dollars. An accountant can look at Insook's hair salons and say how much income she's produced over the past few years. He can even estimate how much she's likely to earn in the next year or so by analyzing customer loyalty and the amount of new business that has come in over the past couple of years. The accountant then follows a formula to put a dollar amount on the good will Insook has built up over the years. The ability of an accountant to use a formula to figure out how loyal Insook's customers are and how the business is growing might come as a surprise to you. This good will part of the business has a dollar value.

Different Ways to Divide a Business

Sometimes one party buys the other party out. For example, in the case study Insook might have to pay her ex-husband for his share of the businesses. Or maybe he gets the house and the 401(k), and Insook gets the hair salons. That way she could then own the hair salons alone. However, that's not always possible, especially if the amount owed to one person is quite large, or if the business has a lot of debt and there's not much money available for a payoff. This becomes a big problem if the couple has no other assets to balance out one party taking the family business.

The court will usually only order a business to be sold as a last resort. If at all possible, the court will try to find a way for one party to hold onto his or her livelihood. But if the parties can't decide an equitable way to divide a business, the court will step in and do so.

Debts

The main type of debt in most divorces is a mortgage, a car loan, or credit card debt. Usually the person who gets the house also takes on the responsibility for the mortgage, so that debt is awarded to him or her. The same is true with cars; whoever gets the car gets the debt.

When debt is divided, it is put in the name of the person who will ultimately be responsible. So if one person gets the house and the home mortgage, he or she will typically have to refinance the mortgage to remove the other party from the debt. This can pose a problem if the person who is taking the home cannot qualify for a mortgage in his or her name alone.

In some cases the parties will negotiate to delay the removal of one party from the mortgage debt. This most often happens in friendly divorces when the parties agree that the children should stay in the family home, and the parent who has custody cannot afford to refinance the house until he or she gets back on his or her feet financially. However, the other parent must be careful when agreeing to this, because when someone's name already appears on one mortgage, they may not qualify for an additional mortgage on a different home. Distribution of debt, especially the home mortgage, is the kind of thing that must be carefully considered in a divorce settlement. Most good lawyers will help the parties work through this issue to prevent unpleasant surprises later on.

In some states the spouse who signed the credit card application may be held responsible for the credit card debt with his or her name on it. If the family charged up "family" debt, however, the couple may be jointly liable, even if only one name is on the credit application or the credit card. If both parties signed the application, they are usually both responsible—even if one party does not know the other one ran up the bill. In community-property states it doesn't matter who charged up the card or whose name is on the card; the debt will usually be shared equally.

Now you can see why it's important for you to know how debt is divided in your state. If you have credit card debt, the laws of your state will determine who will be responsible. And as always, if you can't agree on who pays for which debt, the courts will decide for you.

What Do You Think?

- Look at the asset list you wrote in chapter 3. Did you include any businesses owned (in part or whole) by you or your spouse? Can you put a value on these assets or estimate how much they're worth? Can you put a value on customer loyalty to these businesses? How do you think the assets would be divided if you broke up?

- What about the debts on your list from chapter 3? Do you think it's fair for both spouses to be responsible for the debts generated by each spouse separately? What if the wife did not know the husband was charging up thousands of dollars worth of collectible trains? Should she be liable for that debt?

- You have a friend who is very attached to her house. What advice can you give her if she insists she should get the house in her upcoming divorce? Why should she contact a mortgage broker early on in the process?

- Think about the question of whether one party should get more than 50 percent of the assets. Should it be the person who makes more money? Or should it be the person who earns lower wages? Take both sides of this argument and explain why each side makes sense. (Hint: Try taking the position of a spouse who moved around the country and lost job opportunities so that the other spouse could advance his or her career.)

5 Who Gets the Kids? Custody Questions

This is probably the hottest issue in a divorce dispute or when unmarried parents break up. And it could be the most painful one, because breakups affect kids for a long time. No one will tell you that every divorce or breakup is bad for every kid. Sometimes it's better to take a child out of a bad situation, but be ready. It's not an easy process.

The Best Interests of the Children

You're going to hear this phrase—"the best interests of the children"—a lot in the *Your Rights in Divorce and Child Custody: Legal Guide*. That's because one of the most important job of a court in a custody or divorce proceeding is to look out for the kids. Whenever there is any kind of question that affects minor children in a divorce, the courts must consider their needs first and foremost.

KEY POINT

It's also important to remember that it's really not a question, these days, of one parent or the other "getting the kids." Most courts recognize that kids need to stay connected with both parents. So the goal is to keep both

Mom and Dad in a child's life and still give that child a stable home with a space of his or her own, a place that is familiar and safe every day. In some states the courts have begun to use the term "residential time" instead of "visitation" so that the parent who does not have primary custody is still seen as a full parent.

If the Parents Can't Agree, the Court Gets Involved in a Big Way

It's a scary thought to realize that a court might tell us how to raise our kids. But that may be how it feels when a divorcing couple has to have the courts decide who has custody and who pays child support. There are other questions too: Who makes decisions for the children when they're still minors? How often should the child spend time with the other parent? And what about the holidays? Who "gets" Christmas? Every family is different and has its own individual needs and family traditions, so every parenting plan or **child custody plan** should take this into consideration.

Even if the parents never married, the courts will likely require that the children have the benefit of both parents in their lives. Custody arrangements do not only happen during a divorce process.

You've heard this suggestion before: it's much better for everyone if you can agree on the terms of **child custody** without fighting about it at all. In fact, this happens most of the time. If you can agree between yourselves, the court won't have to get involved in the private details of your family life. One thing lawyers often say is that a good compromise leaves both parties a bit unhappy.

That means they each gave in to the other side enough to feel upset. A compromise agreement may not mean each party is happy with the outcome, but it's usually better than going to court.

If you're doing your own divorce, or creating a parenting plan without the help of a lawyer for a child born to unmarried parents, it's a very good idea to learn as much as you can about the local laws before you start the process. And remember: This guide is only an educational tool; it cannot provide accurate legal advice that will apply to each unique situation.

TAKE NOTE

It's important to know that even if you don't have a lawyer, you're still required to follow all court rules and requirements, just as any lawyer would. Luckily there is a lot of help out there for people getting divorced without lawyers. Many states and many cities have legal aid societies. And there are free or low-cost legal clinics or legal education centers where you can get good information. Here's just one example, in Washington state: the Northwest Women's Law Center (www.nwwlc.org).

RESOURCES

Custody Statutes

Each state has its own set of laws, or statutes, about child custody. These laws are based on serving the child's best interests. When a court determines custody, it has to look at the facts of the case and then apply the state law. The court must follow the factors set out in the state statutes and determine how those factors apply to each individual case. The court doesn't just get to say, "I like the mom better, so she wins." In this chapter we'll look at the typical factors most states include in their statues, but

TAKE NOTE

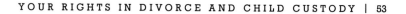

remember that every state is different, so check out the laws that apply to you.

This means that the law for you, where you live, might be different than where your sister or cousin lives, in anther state. If she calls you for advice about her divorce, it's a good idea to encourage her to learn about the custody laws in her state first, before she takes any steps. For example, before she moves out and leaves the kids with their father, she should figure out what could happen to her custody rights. She may have a hard time later proving that she is the best primary parent in a divorce proceeding.

Kinds of Custody

There are different terms for the ways parents share the responsibilities of parenting after a divorce. How those choices are made is part of the divorce process, and we'll talk about that process in chapter 11. A couple of new terms are used in this chapter: in many states the parent who has the children most of the time is often called the "custodial parent," and the other parent is often called the "noncustodial parent." Other states have different terms, but the idea is the same.

KEY POINT

Here's an important thing to know about parenting after a divorce: even if one parent does not have primary custody, or does not have an equal amount of parenting time with the children, most states allow (and even encourage) the noncustodial parent to stay as involved in the child's life as possible. A noncustodial parent may become the coach of his child's sports team or the troop leader of her child's scout troop. Some noncustodial parents regularly volunteer in the child's classroom or go along on field trips. This way, the noncustodial parent has a chance to interact with the child even during time that is technically not his or her custodial time under the parenting plan.

Let's review the two most common kinds of custody: There is "primary custody" and "**joint custody**." "Primary custody" means that the children live with one parent and have regular visits, often frequent or long ones, with the other parent. Both parents should remain involved in major decisions regarding their child, but one parent has most of the day-to-day responsibilities for that child. Do you know someone whose son or daughter visits on every other weekend and Wednesday nights for dinner? That might be an example of the other parent having primary custody.

"Joint custody" is another term you're apt to hear. In this arrangement both parents share the routine responsibilities and decisions about parenting, and the child should have a space of his or her own in each parent's home. You might know someone who has his kids three days a week and on alternating weekends; that's most likely a joint custody arrangement.

The Custody Arrangement

If you look back at the case study, you'll see that Insook got very upset when her attorney told her about the parenting plan. (Some states call the custody arrangement the "parenting plan"; others call it the "child custody plan"; and still others just include it as part of the final divorce decree.) The plan for the kids is one of the most important aspects of a divorce. The custody arrangement deals with two basic parts: First is where the kids will live. Second is what kind of visiting rights the noncustodial parent will have.

KEY POINT

In order to determine which parent should be the **primary residential parent**, many states have guidelines that ask which parent did the majority of the parenting functions for the children. These include things like who deals with the day-to-day realities of the children: who helps with their daily routine, gets them up, makes breakfast, takes them to school, takes them to the doctor, organizes their activities, helps with homework, and so on. You can see that the guidelines for primary custody look at the details of a family's life. So in a custody dispute the court will have to evaluate a lot of highly personal information about the family. This is never a nice process, and it's the main reason why most people try hard to settle their custody disagreements without going to court.

Making Decisions Together

Most states now recommend joint decision-making, even when the child lives primarily with one parent. The idea here is that both parties should have equal input on decisions about what school the child attends, what doctor he or she goes to, and so on. In cases of domestic violence or similar difficult custody issues, the courts will probably not require joint decision-making. In fact, some states will not even allow the parties to agree to joint decision-making in cases of domestic violence unless there is a very good explanation. Again, this makes sense. If the parties' relationship is too hostile, they aren't likely to get along well enough to make decisions together.

Coming up with a Parenting Plan
or Child Custody Plan

When the parties are in the process of deciding a parenting plan and can't agree, it's a good idea for them to use the same criteria a court would use to decide on a parenting plan. That way, they can hopefully avoid a trial, since the plan they come up with is something close to how a court would rule anyway. Keep in mind that if you and your spouse come to an agreement on your own, you don't have to follow any state guidelines. The guidelines are just there if the parties can't agree. Here are some questions most courts think about when they create a parenting plan for children in a divorce:

- Which parent did most of the parenting jobs during the year before the separation?
- What kind of relationship is there between the parents, siblings, and others who are important to the child?
- How well adjusted are the children to their home, school, church, and community?
- What's the mental health of each person in this situation?
- What does the child want, assuming he or she is old enough to understand the choices?
- Are there specific religious and cultural considerations?

- How can the court best provide a continued stable home environment for the child?
- What connections can the child have with extended family?
- What is the age and gender of the child?
- Are there concerns about the parents regarding severe discipline or emotional abuse?
- Is there any evidence of drug, alcohol, or sexual abuse?

Now that you've seen this list of things a court considers, think of how they would fit in some specific situations. Sit back in the judge's chair and apply these facts to the four scenarios listed below to see how you would rule. Can you see why a judge might consider the answers to each question important?

- *Scenario 1.* Mom was in the Army Reserves and was gone all the time. In fact, that was one issue that led to Mom and Dad's divorce. Now Mom wants full custody of her son and daughter.
- *Scenario 2.* Fifteen-year-old Sally has some trouble with depression and sees a counselor. Her counselor believes the planned joint custody arrangement isn't a good idea for Sally.
- *Scenario 3.* Dad moved out after a big fight with Mom. Mom argues that Dad is never home, that he's always working. She says that she is the primary parent of their two-year-old daughter, Julie, since she has to take the baby to day care and pick her up every day. What other information would the court need to make a decision about primary custody in this case?
- *Scenario 4.* Mom has two children from her first marriage, and now she wants custody of the child she has with her second husband. He says he is very involved

in the son's daily activities and should have primary custody. Of what importance, if any, is the little boy's relationship with his half-siblings?

What If the Parties Can't Agree on a Custody Arrangement?

Often the parties have different ideas of what would be the best plan for their children after the divorce. What then? How can a court make this kind of decision when it doesn't know the family and doesn't have time during a short trial to gather all of the information necessary to make this important decision? Typically, in these situations the court appoints a person to gather information about the family and present it to the court. The two most common ways to do this are by a parenting evaluation, or by appointing a **guardian *ad litem***, who is often a lawyer or mental health professional, to represent the best interests of the child.

KEY POINT

Sometimes Child Protective Services (CPS) gets involved, but that is less common. The name of this government service might be different from state to state, but the goals are the same: to protect children from dangerous or unhealthy home situations.

Parenting Evaluators

In a parenting dispute, often each parent thinks he or she is the one best suited to be the primary parent. In these cases the court needs help in determining just what the best plan for the kids really is. The court may appoint a mental health professional or an experienced family law lawyer to make a recommendation. This person, the

parenting evaluator, is trained in child development and in mental health issues. He or she may even be a professional counselor. The parenting evaluator's job is to use the state guidelines to determine which parent is the one who best fits the role of primary parent according to the state laws.

He or she interviews both the father and the mother. Then the parenting evaluator talks to the children about their family life. The evaluator looks at lots of different things in the way a parent deals with a child. The evaluator often interviews other people who see the parents and children together, such as a day-care provider, grandparents, teachers, or neighbors. The parents usually have to answer a long list of questions. Sometimes this is called a **parenting history survey**. The goal of this survey is to find out which parent has been fulfilling the role of primary parent as defined by the particular state statute and to make a recommendation to the court.

At the end of the evaluation, the parenting evaluator writes a report that sets out his or her findings. When the parenting evaluation is complete, a case can often be settled out of court, since the court almost always goes along with the recommendations of the parenting evaluator. But sometimes the parties disagree with the findings and opinion of the parenting evaluator and want to go to court. When this happens, the parenting evaluator makes a recommendation to the court, and the parties challenge the recommendation by questioning the parenting evaluator in court. When one party does not like the recommendation, questioning the evaluator in court is called "cross-examination."

KEY POINT

What If the Parents Can't Get Along Well Enough to Be Civil with Each Other When Transferring the Kids?

When there is lots and lots of conflict, a parenting evaluator may recommend that the parents exchange the children at a **neutral exchange site**, like a church or social services center. A neutral exchange site is a place that is less likely to create emotional upset for either the parents or the kids. This way Dad and Mom can go to the same place and wait in their cars while the children walk between them. When the parents have this much trouble getting along, it's always bad for the children. That's why it's best not to let divorce situations become so hotly contested if at all possible. Of course, in cases of domestic violence, it's not usually possible to avoid conflict.

What If I Move to Another State? The Uniform Child Custody Jurisdiction and Enforcement Act (UCCJEA)

The Uniform Child Custody Jurisdiction and Enforcement Act (UCCJEA) is an important law that talks about children of divorce and custody issues when there are different states involved. It explains which state has the power to make decisions about a child custody situation and what to do if you have moved to a new state and want to change your custody arrangement.

STATUTE

The UCCJEA gives careful explanations about what is considered a child's "home state." It also makes clear that the home state has the final say, or jurisdiction, over child custody questions. In the case study, for example, if Andy

had moved to another state, that state would not necessarily have any say in the children's custody arrangements. If a court case were to be filed, the first thing the
court would have to determine is which state is the child's
"home state." That state would have the power to make
rulings about the children. The other state would then
have to honor those custody decisions.

Then there's the question of modifying, or changing,
custody arrangements. Under the UCCJEA another state
can't modify the arrangements approved by the child's
home state, unless the home state decides that it no longer
holds jurisdiction. That could happen if the family members move to another state, but there are risks involved
if a parent moves his or her child without considering
the custody rights of the other parent. The best way to
prevent problems is to do your homework about custody
before you decide to move. This is called "relocation" in
most states and is discussed in the next section.

TAKE NOTE

Let's look at this example: Maybe your cousin, who
lived in Nebraska, got a divorce and his ex-wife has custody of their child. He's moved out to Oregon for a better job, and his son visits him for six weeks. Your cousin
can't go to court in Oregon to change his son's custody
arrangement; the Nebraska courts have that job, and the
Oregon courts would have to follow the rulings of the
Nebraska courts.

Sometimes there are difficult or even dangerous situations that need special attention. That might be the case
with domestic violence or kidnapping, for example. The
UCCJEA makes it possible for a court to issue emergency
orders to protect a child. But be warned: This is *not* a way

to get back at your ex or to get around a custody arrangement you don't like. There have to be good reasons for such a request, and it's complicated.

You can read more about this important child protection statute by typing in UCCJEA into a good Web search engine, or visiting www.law.upenn.edu and searching the site for the act.

RESOURCES

What If I Want to Move and Take My Kids?

Let's say a couple has been divorced for five years. Things are going along okay. Child support is regular. The kids have adjusted to the different kind of family. Both parents have decent jobs. Then a new issue comes up: Mom or Dad gets a job promotion. Great news, but it means a move away from their home community. Or maybe one parent wants to remarry, and again, a move is part of the plan. What's the big deal, right?

This is what courts and divorce lawyers refer to as "relocation," and it can be a big deal. If the parties can't agree on whether the kids should be able to move, the courts may have to get involved again. There are strict rules in most states about when a child of divorce can be moved from the community where she or he is currently living. Again, the best solution is to check out the rules where you live before you do anything. Often the rule is that when the primary parent wants to move the child out of the school district, he or she needs the other parent's agreement. So you should let your ex know what you're thinking about. If he's okay with the plan, things can proceed smoothly, but if he disagrees, you have to follow your state laws regarding moving.

TAKE NOTE

Wait a minute! Can the courts really tell you that you can't take that good job promotion in another state? No, that's not the message here. The courts in most states won't tell an adult where he or she may live. But in a divorce the courts can decide where the *child* is to live. Some states have a checklist of relocation factors that are similar to the factors used to figure out which parent should be the primary parent. It's important to check the rules in the state where you live.

If you decide to move yourself and your child anyway, you could be charged with something called "**custodial interference**," or taking a child without permission. Custodial interference happens when one parent moves the child in violation of the custody plan and without the permission of the other parent. This is obviously not the same thing as kidnapping, but it is considered a crime in most states. If the parent takes the child to another state, the UCCJEA applies to give the court in the new state the power to follow the ruling of the child's home state and order the child back home. All of these laws fit together like a puzzle to protect the child's best interests.

TAKE NOTE

It's Just Another Country, and It's Only an Airplane Flight Away

Here's an interesting problem in child custody cases that is becoming more common. It involves children whose parents hold passports from different countries, and international law is important here. Look at this example: A couple splits up after five years of marriage. They have one child. The wife holds an American passport, and so does their small daughter.

The husband was born and raised in Spain. He wants to head back home, but what about the child? The courts have awarded Mom primary custody, but Dad decides to take the child anyway. He figures once she's home with him in Spain everything will settle down, and besides, once he's out of the United States, what can the courts do, anyway? A lot. He should have done his homework. An important international agreement called the Hague Convention comes into play here. The 1996 Hague Convention entered into force on January 1, 2002.

STATUTE

The Hague Convention covers a lot of different topics. But in the case of child custody, it says that all countries who signed on to the agreement, referred to as the "Convention," agree to follow the custody rulings of a child's home country. So the court in Spain will follow the parenting plan that was entered in the U.S. state court. The Spanish court should therefore order that the little girl be sent back home to live with her mother in the United States.

You're right! It's not always that simple. What if a country hasn't signed on to the Hague Convention? Several countries haven't. (You can find out which ones haven't signed on. Just choose a good search engine on the Web and type in a phrase like "Hague Convention + child custody." These include some countries in Central Asia, such as Afghanistan, India, and Pakistan.) Here's a Web site to check for this type of information: <u>www.usdoj.gov</u>.

RESOURCES

Let's look at a second example, and it is easy to imagine how painful this story can be. Dad is an American, and Mom is from India, a country that isn't a member of the Hague Convention. She knows nobody checks passports when the child gets on the plane with her, and once she's off the plane in her home country, who's going to be able to find that child? What's more, the government of that country won't help the United States in its efforts to get the child back to the father. Colombia, El Salvador, Thailand, and Zimbabwe are just a few of the other countries that don't agree to the terms of the Hague Convention.

TAKE NOTE

Could this story be yours? If it is, you have some options. Take two simple but important steps: Get your child a passport and lock it up in a safe place. Or notify the State Department to flag the passport—to take special notice if someone tries to use it. If you believe your spouse is planning to leave the country with your child, you should seek legal advice immediately; this is one situation where it's very important to act quickly.

Third-Party Custody

Third-party custody is a less common solution that happens in a divorce situation, or even when there is not divorce but when there are reasons why neither parent is considered suitable to raise children. There may be drug use. There may be criminal activity on the part of one or both parents. But it's not easy for a third party, such as a grandparent, to obtain custody.

TAKE NOTE

Let's look at this example: Mom is in prison, and Dad is doing drugs. The grandparents want to take the kids out of an ugly situation. What can they do? In most states they have to prove to the courts that the parent or parents are not able to do the job. (This is another example of when or why Child Protective Services could get involved.)

Does this mean the parent loses his or her parental rights forever? That's not usually the case. Often the parent can come back into the picture. If he or she can show that the problems are resolved, through counseling or drug treatment, for example, the parent can seek to regain custody of the child. The court has a tough standard to meet. You already know the phrase: "the best interests of the child."

A Word about Grandparents' Rights

There are plenty of legal cases that give parents visitation rights with their kids after a divorce. But the same is not true with grandparents. In fact, this is an interesting area of the law that was recently addressed by the United States Supreme Court. It is very unusual for the Supreme Court to address a family law issue, but that's what happened in the *Troxel v. Granville* (2000) case.

In this case grandparents wanted more visitation rights with their grandchildren after their son, the children's father, had died. The children's mother agreed to visits but not as often as the grandparents had wanted. The Court said that the mother's basic right to make decisions for her children included how often they could see their paternal grandparents. The Court said that the grandparents had no visitation rights. The Court clearly gave more weight to the parent than to the grandparents, and that's why this case was so important.

My Kids Aren't Taking
This Divorce Thing Very Well

If you're a parent thinking about getting a divorce, or you are an unmarried parent thinking about a breakup, you'll be smart to learn a little about how the breakup can affect kids. Having this knowledge can actually make the whole process easier for you, not just for them.

In many families there is plenty of fighting before a breakup. Sometimes there's physical abuse, drug or alcohol abuse, maybe even sexual abuse. There might be gambling debts, or fears about losing the family home. Sometimes a new boyfriend or girlfriend complicates the picture. Many trained professionals—teachers, counselors, psychologists, and clergy—have spent a lot of time and training so they can help kids through a divorce. This section offers a sample of what they've learned.

Kids have different emotional reactions to divorce depending on their age. A preschool child might miss his dad a lot if he lives with mom, but if his life is stable and safe, that will help a lot. A fourteen-year-old boy, however, has lots of questions and worries. He may think he did something wrong and that's why his mom left. Or he may blame his dad for driving his mother away. Young adults, who may be in close relationships themselves, have another whole set of questions, like whether marriage is even a good idea. After all, their own parents couldn't make their marriage work, right?

Here are some other things to watch out for: kids may be more afraid after their parents split up, especially younger children. Many of them can't understand how Dad stopped loving Mom; could he stop loving the child too? They may not want to be separated from their parent, so going to school and daycare can be hard for parents and kids both. There may be less money—sometimes a lot less—for things like school clothes, movies, and things that kids want to do with their friends. The kids in a divorce may have to be alone more often, if their parent is working longer hours. Sometimes boys who live without much contact with their fathers have more discipline problems. Older kids, teenagers especially, may have trouble with depression.

Don't assume all these discouraging things will happen in your family. But it's better to know about the custody laws before you start the process, and it's a really good idea to be prepared to help your kids long before you file papers to start a divorce or custody case.

So What Can I Do?

There's a long list of problems that kids could have after a divorce. But parents should remind themselves that their kids don't have to have these problems. There are plenty of ways to help your kids, or your grandkids, or your nieces and nephews, if they're going through a divorce.

The first thing to remember is that it might be better for your child to be in a divorced family. Staying in a household where there is constant arguing, for example, isn't any good for your kids either. So everything you do from now on can be an improvement for your child.

Another important thing you can do if you are the non-custodial parent is to stay involved in your child's life. Go to parent-teacher conferences, even if you've had a long work day and you know it won't be an easy conference. Go to school activities. Find a church or a community center that has kid-friendly activities, especially ones that include a parent and child together. Many nonresidential parents find ways to see their children during times that the children are scheduled to be with the other parent by coaching sports teams, leading scout troops, or

TAKE NOTE

volunteering for school activities like field trips or other events. In time, the other parent may come to appreciate the help with driving to sports or other activities. The key is not to be pushy.

Listen to what your child's worries and fears are. Don't tell him or her that those fears are silly, or that you have problems of your own. After all, you're the adult here. Instead, let your child know that you understand, that you're working to make things better, and that everything will be okay.

Parenting Classes

TAKE NOTE

It's not easy being a parent. Any parent will tell you that. If you really don't know what to do or where to turn, check with social services in your community. Most cities and many counties have some kind of **parenting classes** available. Some of them are through the local community college. A parenting class can do several things for you: You meet other people dealing with the same stresses, so it can help you. You learn some new ways of helping your kids so their behaviors don't make life harder for you. If the courts are involved in sorting out your divorce, or if your child has a guardian *ad litem*, taking a parenting class shows that you are serious about being a good parent.

What Do You Think?

- Talk to someone with kids who's going through a divorce. Find out how the parenting plan affects the family.
- Do you think grandparents should have visitation

rights with their grandchildren after a divorce?

- Your friend at work has parents who live in another country, and she's thinking about divorcing and taking her child back to her parents. What would you suggest she do first?

- Every week there's something in the news about a divorce that involves children. Notice what's in the news for one month. How many variations on the question of child custody did you hear or read about?

- Your neighbors are getting a divorce, and you think their ten-year-old kid is getting lost in the middle of some nasty fights. You're worried about his mental health. What are some things you could do?

- Talk to an adult who was a child of divorce. Be sure to respect his or her privacy, but see what this person has to say about the experience and how it affects his or her view of marriage today.

- Your buddy is a recently divorced dad who plans to move to another city for a new job. He wants to take his daughter, but she would have to give up her horse. She says her horse is her best friend. What do you tell him?

- Look at that last question again. Would you change your opinion if the dad will take the horse with him when he moves? What if the mom and the daughter's extended family and all of her friends will be several hours away from the dad's new location?

- A thirteen-year-old has been having trouble at school ever since his parents split up. He's always in trouble. Mom thinks moving to a different city might be the solution, but it would mean a change in visitation rights for Dad. What should Mom do first?

6 Child Support

Y ou might know some divorced parents who love their kids but complain about child support. You might know some single parents who never have enough money to pay all the bills every month. And you might know some kids who are caught in the middle. These are all problems that can follow a divorce. The question of child support can bring up a lot of emotions for people.

Once You Have a Child, You Have a Big Financial Obligation

Children are expensive. We all know that. And it's the parents' obligation to support their children. All U.S. states require both parents to provide financial support to their kids. In fact, the law is so strong on this point that failure to pay child support can cause a parent to lose his or her driver's license and sometimes could even land a parent in jail.

How is child support figured out? In most states there are court-ordered guidelines for the amount of child support. That means the law assigns an amount based on information about both parents' incomes; in most states the law does not allow the court to just pick a number that seems right for each family. The goal of child support is to provide as consistent and stable an environment for the kids as possible. They aren't the ones who got divorced, after all.

But the Other Parent Has to Spend Money on the Kids Too, Right?

Here's an idea that some noncustodial parents have trouble with: Let's say a single mother with two kids has them through the school week and every other weekend. They visit their dad two weekends a month and every Wednesday evening for dinner. He wants to have the kids over more, as much as three nights every week. He wants to spend more time with them, but he's also tired of having the money deducted from his paycheck for child support every month. He figures if he has the kids more each week, he can pay the mother less each month. After all, he's feeding them, taking them to the movies, and they have a bedroom in his place. Different states have different rules about this issue, so this is another instance when you have to check the laws in your state.

KEY POINT

Remember, even if the children spend time with the noncustodial parent, the custodial parent still has to pay the rent or mortgage even on those days the children are not at home. Think of child support as the way to provide your kids with a stable life. Don't think of it as money that goes to your ex. Remember that the kids deserve as much stability as you can provide for them.

Unknown Future Expenses

If a divorcing couple is asked to think about costs ten years down the road, they might think that's a silly idea. But in a divorce some of that long-term thinking has to happen. This is especially the case when kids are involved. Many child support orders include standard language about things like medical expenses. If the divorcing couple has a similar level of income, they will be expected to contribute an amount, based on their income, toward medical costs for their children. This makes sense when you think about how many expensive treatments and tests could suddenly become part of a single parent's life if his or her child has a bad injury or develops a life-threatening disease.

Another routine cost written into a lot of child support orders is educational expenses. Maybe your daughter wants to go to the local private school. If you and your ex don't agree on this, you can go to court and let a judge decide. The judge in this situation will look at the parents' income and the reasons the child wants to go to the school, and weigh the pros and cons. Judges typically do not require parents to pay for expensive things like private school if they have limited income, but if they have the money to pay, the judge may order them to do so.

Child Support When There Are Children but No Marriage

Maybe you know a couple who never got married but has a child. Or maybe the mother got pregnant after a first date. The status of the relationship between the parties doesn't matter. In addition to a custody plan, the child needs to be supported and the parents have to pay.

If you or a friend find yourself in this situation, make sure that both the father's and the mother's names are on the child's birth certificate. If this does not happen at the hospital, it's not too late, but review your state laws on this issue since there may be a time limit within which the father can easily claim paternity. If he waits too long, there is usually a legal proceeding to follow to get this straightened out. Fathers, this is the most important thing you can do if you want to be a part of your child's life. But if a man believes he has been wrongly named as the child's father, he can go to court and ask that the child have a blood test to see if he is the father.

Many states require certain information before the name of an unmarried father goes on a child's birth certificate. These states require the father to sign an **affidavit**. This is a legal document, signed in front of a person authorized to accept the document. In the case of a child's birth, the affidavit says the father acknowledges that he is the child's father. For unmarried mothers this is a good way to protect a child if the father later claims the child is not his. Again, if there is a doubt about who is the father, it is best to rely on DNA testing rather than an affidavit.

TAKE NOTE

Let's look at this from the child's side, too: A father wants his teenage child to get some of his pension in case of the father's death, but the parents never married. There is no document naming the father as a legal parent, so the child is not likely to get any benefits from a pension fund or Social Security.

Failure to Pay Child Support

What happens when the child support checks come for a while, then they stop? What can the custodial parent do? Some states allow **liens** or garnishment against the paycheck of a person behind in child support. A lien is the legal right to hold a portion of a person's property in order to pay a debt or claim. This means that the state can garnish the wages of the person who is obligated to pay child support. Imagine one day seeing hundreds of dollars being taken out of your paycheck! This can happen if you do not pay child support as ordered by the court.

TAKE NOTE

In some states "deadbeat" parents who aren't paying the required child support might lose their driver's license. The state could even put them in jail. Remember that basic duty of the court—to look after the child's best interests. Don't think that women get away from these responsibilities either. In the case study, for example, if Andy got custody of the children, Insook would be expected to pay child support too. If she failed to comply with the court's requirements, it's possible that the court could place a lien against her businesses.

What Do You Think?

• Talk to divorced parents. Find out what things they have to do differently because money is tight.

• Your friend says his ex-wife doesn't spend the child support money he sends her on his kids. He wants to quit sending her money. What do you tell him?

• Lots of fathers feel excluded from their kids' lives and

think the only thing they can do is send money. How could they change that?

- Do you think the father in an unmarried couple should help support the children if the couple splits up?
- A coworker has been divorced for a long time. Now her son wants to go to college and she doesn't agree with his choice, so she doesn't want to help pay for tuition. Does this seem like a good solution to the problem? What are her options?
- What steps could a new mother take to protect her infant, in terms of who his or her father is?
- How can you learn what the rules are where you live for collection of back child support?

7 Alimony or Maintenance

In many divorces one spouse has to pay money every month to the other spouse for a certain period of time. This is different from child support payments. The idea behind this is to support the spouse who didn't work or didn't make as much money during the marriage, while he or she gets back into the workforce. Sometimes the nonworking spouse has to go to school or get another type of training to get a decent job. This monthly payment is called "maintenance" or "alimony".

KEY POINT

Most people think it's just women who get alimony from their ex-husbands. This used to be the most common case, because in the past more women stayed home with the children while the father worked and advanced in his career. Then, when the ex-wife had to start working again, she might have needed some job training or more education to get a decent job. However, these days maintenance can go to either spouse, depending on his or her employment situation. The courts in most states usually limit the time period for which maintenance or alimony is required. The amount of maintenance is often lower than it used to be, and the payments don't go on for as long.

The courts today believe that more women have better ways to support themselves than they used to. But either way the court has the final say.

Another important thing to remember is that in most states alimony is not like child support in that there is no predetermined amount that is required by the state. The court can listen to each individual situation and make the award that it believes is best for that person. When a court does this, it is called "exercising discretion." Since most divorce cases are settled by the parties, the parties can usually figure out a reasonable amount of alimony that they believe a court would order and agree to that amount. This avoids an expensive and painful trial. Once they understand the factors that would be considered by the court, the parties can reach an agreement. Here are types of factors most state laws tell the court to consider:

- The financial situation of both persons
- The length of time the person getting maintenance would need to become self-supporting
- The couple's standard of living when they were married
- The length of the marriage
- The age and physical and emotional health of both people
- The ability of the supporting person to support the other and still support him- or herself fairly

You can see how many things a court must look at when it's a question of maintenance. And you probably know someone who's either getting maintenance (alimony) or paying it. Do you know anyone who's getting or paying it *for life* (this is called "lifetime maintenance")? That happens too, but not so often any more. This happens today most commonly when people get divorced after being married for many years.

The court has to decide not only whether one party should pay maintenance to the other, but also how much and for how long. This means both parties have to give accurate and honest information about how much money they spend monthly, and on what, as well as what their typical earnings are. If one party is dishonest, you can see how complicated the picture gets. Usually the court requires both parties to submit copies of their monthly bills, such as rent and utilities, as well as tax returns and pay stubs.

There's also the problem of trying to predict the future. Both parties are asked to make a fair estimate of how much money they think they'll need to live on in the coming months or years. For a spouse who is just starting back to work, this can be a difficult thing to guess. Here's an example of how complicated maintenance questions can be: let's say that during marriage the couple lived in an expensive part of the country, maybe New York City. After the divorce one partner moved back to his home town in another state where rent, food, and even gas was a lot less expensive. So how much should one spouse pay the other for maintenance when the cost of living changes so much?

The question of physical and emotional health was mentioned earlier. If you've been divorced or you know someone who is going through a divorce, you know the process can be hard on everyone. Maybe one spouse seeks counseling for depression and anxiety as a result of all the changes in his life during and after the divorce.

Does this situation make it impossible for that person to hold a job? How will the courts consider the question of financial support for that person if he claims he can't work?

What Do You Think?

• Your friend is getting a divorce. She has few job skills, though. She hasn't worked in a long time because the couple moved from city to city during the marriage when her husband changed jobs. What are her options?

• Is it fair to ask a fifty-five-year-old who hasn't worked in twenty years to find a job, any job? What are some possible problems with this expectation?

• Do you think the length of time for making alimony payments should be tied to the length of the marriage? Let's say a couple was married for twenty-five years, and the wife didn't work outside the home. She asks for fifteen years of maintenance, and her ex announces he'll take her to court over this request. What information would you need to make a decision if you were the judge in this case?

• Your friend is showing everybody her expensive engagement ring. She announces that she plans to quit her job after she marries. What do you think of this idea? What would you tell her?

• Talk to a few people who have just started back to work after a long time of not working outside the home. Ask them how the work they're doing now compares to what kinds of challenges and responsibilities they had in their earlier jobs.

• Your sister knows she needs to start working again

because the maintenance agreement in her divorce settlement only gives her support for another year. But she's worried that her job skills are very out-of-date. What can she do to get some new job skills for the current job market?

• Your neighbor is on the go all the time for volunteer work. Then she learns her husband is leaving her. She insists her volunteer work is important to her mental health, and says her ex should pay for her to stay in her home and continue her volunteer work. Think of arguments for both sides about the problems this plan would cause.

8 The Practical Side of the Divorce Process: How It All Comes Together

D ivorce can be a complicated thing. And it doesn't help to hear all the horror stories about someone else's awful divorce. You hear expressions like these: "I got taken to the cleaner's by my ex" or "My ex wanted the shirt off my back, and now I don't even get to see my kids." It doesn't have to be that way. How can you avoid those horror stories? Educate yourself about the process.

In this chapter you'll read about the practical steps that every divorce involves. You might decide to hire a lawyer. Or you might be on good terms with your ex and you both feel you would like to go through the process without the added legal expenses of hiring lawyers. Here's one important thing to remember, though: Don't let your best friend from another state tell you how it's done. The laws where he lives are likely to be different than where you are. So the first step is to check out the rules about divorce where you live.

If you're doing your own divorce, it's a good idea to study your state's child support guidelines before you write up the terms of your divorce. You're less likely to have problems that way. Remember that the *Civil Survival Series* is not here to give you accurate legal advice for your specific situation; we just want to help you understand a bit more about how the law works.

The State Has All the Statutes Already

Do you know someone who got divorced without hiring a lawyer? That happens a lot, and one reason for this is because all states have a set of steps to follow for getting a divorce. The rules are already laid out for you. You can easily learn about the statues in your state. Go to the Web and choose your favorite search engine. Then type in "divorce" and the state where you live. You can learn a lot right there. Here's just one sample Web site, for the laws in California: www.leginfo.ca.gov/calaw.html.

RESOURCES

Most states have court-required forms for divorcing couples to use. They may look complicated at first, but if you go to the state Web site, there is helpful information for making sense of these forms. When you're using the legal system without a lawyer you are called "pro se." This means you are representing yourself.

Should you talk to a lawyer before you divorce? It's a good idea, so you can learn about the process. There are terms and rules you need to know about. You'll need to learn what kind of information you have to supply to the courts and the proper forms to use. But what if you can't afford an attorney? Or maybe you and your spouse are able to work out the details of property and custody without having a fight over every detail. Look around for a legal aid clinic or divorce class where you live. Law schools often have clinics where students are available to give legal advice under the supervision of a lawyer. There is also a lot of information online. Most counties and states have informational Web sites to help you understand the laws in your state.

TAKE NOTE

Do We Have to Go to Court?

This can be a little confusing. First you hear that it's a good idea to settle a divorce out of court. Then you read that the final papers have to be entered in court. So which is it? How does the system work? The first thing to remember is that the system in your state may work differently from the systems in other states. And some counties even have their own local rules. But here's the basic idea, and most states have something similar.

Let's use Insook and Andy from the case study as examples. Let's say they decided not to hire attorneys. They knew the marriage was over, but they weren't so angry at each other any more. Andy and Insook were able to come to an agreement about the distribution of their assets and decided on a parenting plan. They wrote up an agreement about their property, custody, child support, and visitation rights. Then they down-loaded the correct legal forms for their state from their county Web site. This way their agreement was in the legal form required by their state.

Once these forms were completed, they were pre-sented to the court. A judge or a commissioner checked them over, especially the part about child support, to see that the children were protected. Then the papers were "entered"—that means they were signed by a judge or court commissioner and then filed in the court—and the divorce was finalized. The court had the final say, but it didn't change anything that Insook and Andy had agreed on.

The same thing could happen if Insook and Andy had used **mediation** or **arbitration**. You'll learn about those methods of settling a divorce later in this chapter. Once the mediator helps the parties come up with an agreement, the agreement has to be put in the proper format and entered in court; so once again, the court has the final say.

Most states have clear guidelines about child support. So if a couple like Insook and Andy had come up with a plan that was a lot different than what the state suggested, the court might not agree.

Should I Hire an Attorney?

This could be one of the most important questions early in your divorce process. There are things to consider before you decide whether to pay for legal representation. Consider these questions:

- Is there a lot of property to divide?
- Are there complicated issues regarding the children?
- Is the divorcing couple on speaking terms?
- Can the parties work together toward a compromise?
- How expensive are attorneys' fees for divorce?

If you do decide that an attorney is right in your situation, you need to do some thinking before you hire someone. Don't just pick a name out of the phone book, and don't hire someone just because your friend used that lawyer and got a big settlement. That might not be the best solution in your own case.

Attorneys have different styles, just like any other professionals. Some are more aggressive, like the attorney Andy talked to in the case study, and their approach may be to go to court to resolve disagreements instead of negotiating. Others know a lot about developing good parenting plans and are aware of how divorce affects kids. Some attorneys recognize the stress of a divorce and encourage the clients to compromise. Others fan the flames of anger and try to create more disagreements. And we all know that this can cost a lot of money.

It's important to find an attorney who listens to your needs and follows your wishes as far as the law permits. You might ask an attorney some questions like these: What is the average size of the estate that you handle in divorce cases? How do you go about developing a parenting plan? How can you help me figure out the best custody plan for my children? What can you do to help me stay on speaking terms with my ex? How often do you take a divorce case into court? What are your thoughts on mediation and **alternative dispute resolution**?

TAKE NOTE

There are many more questions that would be good to ask an attorney before you hire him or her. In any case all these questions should have one thing in common: they shouldn't be "yes" or "no" questions. Instead, ask questions that require the attorney to explain his or her views clearly. That way you can get a better idea of whether you like the style of this attorney and whether you can work with him or her.

Starting the Divorce Process:
Filing for Divorce

Let's start at the beginning to see how everything we've learned so far fits together. To start the process, one person has to file a document in court. In most states this is called a "petition for **dissolution of marriage**." A **petition** or complaint is a formal request. In a divorce proceeding, it must be written and has to be in the form recognized by each individual state. You can get a divorce or complaint form online or at your local library or courthouse. Of course if you hire a lawyer, he or she will draft and file your legal documents for you. Legal aid clinics can also provide the forms that are right for your state. You must file this petition with the court and have it properly served on the other party.

TAKE NOTE

As we learned in chapter 4, once the petition or complaint is filed, the court has jurisdiction over the parties. This means that either party can go to court and ask the court to make decisions about how things will be until the final settlement is reached or the case goes to trial. But don't worry, most people simply file the petition to start the process and never go to court until it's time to enter the final paperwork.

Let's look at this process through the eyes of Insook and Andy in the case study. Maybe they both agreed that a divorce was the right solution for them. Still, one of them had to start the process. Insook filed a petition with the court with the help of her attorney. Then Andy was served with a copy of this petition. What's in this petition? It announces the basic facts of the marriage, such as the legal names of both parties and any minor children. It usually lays out the requests of the **petitioner**—that's Insook—in terms of a parenting plan, property division, and any financial support. In most cases the petitioner, or **plaintiff**, can say that these issues should be decided later; they don't have to have all the answers at the beginning of the process.

Service of Process and Response

Suppose Insook and Andy were still on speaking terms, and they were trying to look after their kids too. The petitioner (in this case Insook) would still have to show proof that Andy was notified about the divorce petition. That's what the **service of process** means—Andy was served with a copy of the petition. Then Andy must respond. In most states the person who responds is called the **respondent** or **defendant**.

The respondent (Andy) must file his response to Insook's petition in court within a certain time period. Each state is different, so it's important to check out the deadlines in your state. In some states the petitioner has to serve the respondent with paperwork setting out the deadlines. This is helpful to the respondent in figuring out what has to be done and by when.

Temporary Orders

If Andy and Insook can be civil about their breakup, they probably won't need to request **temporary orders** from the court. But if every discussion leads to a fight, the court may have to step in. The reason these are called temporary orders is that they only last until the final settlement or trial. It's just the way the family lives while they sort out how the divorce will turn out. One thing to keep in mind, though, is that often the situation ordered by the court in a temporary orders hearing is fairly close to the way the final divorce turns out. So it's important to take the temporary situation seriously.

TAKE NOTE

Another fact to take into consideration in filing temporary orders is that whatever you file in court becomes public record. Many people do not think this through before filing. If you file for temporary orders in most states, all of these private matters will be in the court file for anyone to see. You might not worry about this at first, but think about this: it's common for employers to do a background search on people applying for jobs. Do you really want a potential employer to have this kind of personal information about you? And what happens when your child becomes old enough to access the court file online? Or their friends do? You can see that you should think long and hard before filing a motion in court.

To start the temporary order process, one person has to file a motion in court. A motion is the legal term for making a request to the court, so a motion is the way we ask the court to make a ruling. One party files a motion, the other party answers, and often the first party gets to reply to the other person's response. So in the case of Andy and Insook, one party, say it's Andy, would file a motion for temporary orders. Suppose he filed because both he and Insook each thought they should be the primary parent and that the other parent should have to move out. Andy might file a motion for temporary orders asking the court to order the following: that Insook move out of the family home, that she help Andy pay the mortgage on the family home, that she pay temporary child support, and that she have the children every other weekend and every Wednesday night. Insook might respond that Andy should move out and that he should pay child support. Let's say she also expected help with the mortgage from him and wanted Andy to have a visitation schedule with the children.

Now you can see how all of the information you learned about in the earlier chapters comes together: both parties would use the state guidelines to make their argument. We reviewed the typical state guidelines for custody in chapter 6. Both parties would get statements from friends and family members to support their position as to who should be the primary parent and who should live in the family home. Each person discusses the factors in the statute and how he or she believes they apply to the family. Unfortunately, in order for one person to get custody, he or she usually has to criticize the other. You can see how this could get messy, and how you wouldn't want this kind of mudslinging in the public record.

The parties also submit financial information like tax returns, the mortgage statement, or the rental agreement for the family home as well as copies of their pay stubs and the family bills. It's a lot of paperwork to go to court, but the court needs actual proof of all this information to make the best decision. At the hearing on the motion for temporary orders, the court will do its best to figure out in the limited time is has (usually around fifteen minutes!) what the best solution for the family is.

The court decides on a temporary parenting plan that says who should live in the family home, who should move out, and what the visitation schedule should be. The court uses the factors outlined in chapter 6 to make this decision. The court orders temporary child support based on the income shown on the pay stubs submitted by the parties. You'll remember this from chapter 7.

The court evaluates the family finances and decides who pays what bills and who pays temporary alimony (maintenance). This decision is based on the financial information, such as bills and rental agreements, submitted by both parties.

Often at this hearing the court realizes that if the case ends up in court, the trial judge will need lots of information about the family to determine a final **custody arrangement**, so the judge at the temporary orders hearing might appoint a parenting evaluator, which we learned about in chapter 6.

KEY POINT

You can see that temporary orders make sure that the kids are looked after, that bills are paid, that the couple knows who's living in the family home, and so on. These orders usually stay in place until the divorce is final. One thing to know about temporary orders is that the parties can actually agree to these orders, so it is not always necessary to go to court. Some people even agree to hire a parenting evaluator without going to court.

Discovery

Some marriages end with all the facts on the table. Both spouses know how much debt they have, how much property they have, and exactly where the kids will be living. But often one spouse does not have a clear picture of the couple's finances. Maybe they don't know the bank the other person uses, or they don't know what credit cards they have. When this happens, either party can start the legal **discovery** process.

"Discovery" is the legal term for how both sides in a legal dispute work to gather all the facts. You might be asked to provide copies of your bank or credit card statements or your pay stubs. It is common to ask for the parties' retirement statements, including any pension plan information. This provides a complete understanding of all the parties' assets.

TAKE NOTE

There are three main ways this financial information can be formally obtained. One is by sending **interrogatories**, which are questions that must be answered under oath. The second way is by **deposition**; this is when a person is summoned to give sworn testimony under oath in front of a court reporter. It involves answering lawyers' questions. The third and final way is to send a **subpoena**, which is a formal legal document that is sent to the bank or credit card company or the other party's employer. It requires that a company or bank supply the requested information. Anyone who is served with a subpoena should take it very seriously. A subpoena can require you to attend court, to testify, or to send information that the court, or an attorney, needs to completely evaluate a case.

Remember earlier when we discussed the idea of jurisdiction? This idea is important in the discovery process because neither party has the legal right to use legal tools just discussed unless the court has jurisdiction. In order to use these discovery tools, you have to have a petition for dissolution or a complaint already filed. That's what gives the court jurisdiction, and the court needs jurisdiction to enforce these legal discovery tools.

Alternative Dispute Resolution

It's easy to see why settling a divorce out of court is usually the best way to go. For starters, it costs a lot less. It's also likely to be less painful for the entire family. And in most states settling a divorce out of court happens a lot faster, so the family members can get on with their lives.

You read about mediation in the case study. Let's look at this idea, along with the idea of arbitration, more carefully. These options fall under the term "alternative dispute resolution," sometimes referred to as ADR. Settling a divorce by means of alternative dispute resolution is happening a lot more often these days. One reason is because court calendars are so crowded and waiting for a court date to finalize a divorce could drag things out way too long.

KEY POINT

Another important reason to use ADR is that the parties can control the settlement. Often the parties know best what kind of parenting schedule works best for their family. And usually the parties are best suited to decide what is the best way to fairly distribute their property within the specifics of their state laws. Even when the parties strongly disagree, a skilled mediator can help them negotiate a fair resolution to their case. ADR often happens after the discovery process. It's important to have the full facts before settling a case.

So How Long Does It Take, Anyway?

The time it takes to start and complete a divorce is different in every state. Some states have a residency requirement for just filing for divorce. Those states require that you be a resident for a certain amount of time—it's six months in Georgia, for example—before you can even file. Others allow you to file for divorce even if you've only been in the state for a short time. Most states have a waiting period of at least several weeks or months before a divorce is final. This can vary a lot; in some states there is a separation period required for no-fault divorces. Other states simply view all divorces as no-fault and have a waiting period that is the same for all cases. This is another area that is so different from state to state that you should check your own state laws.

Either way it often takes some time to sort through all of the legal issues that have to be decided before a divorce can be finalized. Things like developing a visitation plan can take a lot of time, and the courts want to make sure the kids' best interests are considered. Making decisions about who gets the family home, who is responsible for which debts, and all sorts of other details all take time.

Finally! The Decree of Divorce

In order for a divorce to be final, lots of paperwork is required. And remember, most states have very specific rules about the forms used for the paperwork. The forms usually include many parts. For example, there is the final parenting plan (also called a child custody plan) and a final order of child support. There's a final property settlement agreement, explaining who gets what. And in some states there's also a legal document called "findings of fact and conclusions of law," plus there is the final decree of dissolution. In some states there is only one document, and all of the information is included in that single document. No matter what each state requires, the same issues are typically addressed in the final decree.

KEY POINT

Whatever forms your state requires, they still have to be signed by both parties and presented in court. Once the court has reviewed all the papers involved and signs them, the divorce is granted and is filed at the courthouse. At that point the divorce decree becomes part of the public record. That means the marriage contract is no longer valid, and the two parties are now considered legally single individuals instead of a married couple.

What Do You Think?

- Your best friend is afraid that if she files for divorce, her husband will make a scene in court and accuse her of all sorts of things, like cheating on him. What should she learn about the divorce laws where she lives?

- Why do you think some states require that you live there for several months before you can start divorce proceedings?

- Talk to someone who's recently been divorced. Find out whether he had to go through a discovery process and what information he was asked to provide.

- Now that you've read this chapter, what would you say is the most important thing a person could do before he or she files for divorce?

- Which do you think is better, to have to give reasons (grounds) for divorcing or to have a no-fault divorce?

- Your coworker has moved out and the kids are staying with his wife. What's at least one thing he could do to avoid a hearing for temporary orders from the court?

- Your friend is heading for divorce and asks you what you think about the idea of using a mediator. What do you tell her about the pros and cons of this process?

9 Domestic Violence

The branch of law that deals with marriage and families is called domestic law. That's different from criminal law, but sometimes criminal statutes become a part of the picture. This could happen if there are accusations of violence, stalking, sexual abuse, and many other behaviors between couples, family members, or individuals in a dating relationship. These behaviors often have criminal penalties. They are also considered by the civil court in a family law proceeding. The common term for problems like these is "domestic violence."

Protection Orders, or Restraining Orders

TAKE NOTE

You've probably heard the term "**protection order**" or maybe "**restraining order**." These orders are granted in most states to individuals in "family-like" relationships. They are not only used in divorces, but that is one area where they are often found. Protection orders are used to keep people safe when they believe that another person is likely to harm them. In most states people can go to court and fill out paperwork stating, under oath, that they feel they are in danger. It is important to be very specific when writing the statement for the judge, because the judge will want to know what happened, when, where, and how. If the court finds the testimony believable, and they usually do, the court will sign a temporary protection order. The person who is accused of being dangerous then has an opportunity to appear in court and dispute the charges.

Most states also now have some kind of "domestic violence advocate." These persons are trained to deal with victims of domestic violence, and they can help victims deal with the paperwork that goes along with making charges. It's worth learning these two terms: the "petitioner" or "plaintiff" is the person who asks the court for help and protection. The "respondent" or "defendant" is the person who has to follow the orders of the court, and if he or she doesn't, that person could face criminal charges.

Petitioners can ask for court help if they have good reason to believe they might be harmed by someone who has been close to them. The respondent might be told to have no contact with the petitioner, even by phone. He or she might also be warned not to get within a certain distance, say five hundred feet, of the petitioner or of that person's home, workplace, school, or even children.

KEY POINT

In most states the courts can order emergency parenting plans while a protection order is in place. Court orders can even require the respondent to get treatment for drug or alcohol problems or anger management classes before he or she can earn back the right to visitation with the kids. The respondent is usually also forced to give up any guns or firearms.

Orders like these can last up to a year or longer, and they can be renewed. And here's something interesting: don't think that all the petitioners are women or that all the people who make the threats are men. Plenty of men are victims of domestic violence. And couples in a gay or lesbian relationship can have the same problems. For that matter parents and adult children, or even brothers or sisters, can also be victims of domestic abuse.

Getting a Protection Order

The steps we list in this section are similar around the country but not exactly the same in each state. But remember that you can probably find a domestic violence advocate to help you, if you need it. Someone in your community will know how to connect you to the right resources. Ask at the courthouse, or call the police or your local crisis line. If it's an emergency, dial 911; otherwise call the police department's business office. They'll refer you and you won't have to talk to the police until you're ready.

TAKE NOTE

First you have to fill out a petition or complaint—that's a request—for a court order. Then you'll probably have to appear in front of a judge or court commissioner. You might be able to bring family members, friends, or an advocate with you, but those people will probably not be able to speak to the judge: they're just with you for moral support. During a short hearing, the judge decides whether the court should issue a temporary protection order. The judge usually asks questions about the specifics of your situation. The most important thing the judge is trying to determine is whether you are currently afraid, and if so, why. If the judge decides to grant the protection order, the respondent or defendant is served with the court order, usually by the sheriff's office.

TAKE NOTE

Most states have a procedure that works like this: At the first hearing, if the judge grants the request, she signs a temporary protection order that usually lasts about two weeks, until there can be a hearing to determine whether the order should be made longer; usually up to one year. The temporary order is served on the respondent along with a notification that there will be another hearing in two weeks. At the second hearing, the respondent can come to court and argue that the order should not continue. The judge listens to both sides and decides if there is good cause to issue a one-year order or even a longer one. If an order is entered, the protected party can come back when it expires and ask for it to be extended. There are rules in most states for how to do this, so it's important to find out about the procedure in your state.

Tips for Victims of Domestic Violence

TAKE NOTE

If you're a victim of domestic violence, don't wait to seek help! If you wait too long to ask for help, the judge might not be convinced there really was a problem. And save any evidence, like threatening letters or e-mails or pictures that show physical injury. If you needed medical help as a result of a domestic violence incident, get a copy of the medical treatment that you needed. And *never* make contact yourself with the person who has threatened or hurt you.

Sometimes victims of domestic violence feel bad that they got the other person in trouble with the police. They don't want to testify against that person, and they often think things will get better. But once a charge is made, once you've called the police, it's not all up to you any more. In some states the police or the sheriff have to arrest the person who was accused of violence if they are called to the scene of the violent event.

The prosecuting attorney's office decides whether to make criminal charges, not the victim. Sometimes, even if the victim refuses to testify against the other person, the attorney's office might still file the charges. The reason for this is that often the victim is afraid to testify against the person who has hurt or scared them. And in some relationships the violent one comes back and asks for forgiveness over and over. But in the eyes of the law the violent one has broken the law by hurting the victim, and it is the job of the state to punish people who are accused of a crime.

Many states offer what's called "crime victims' compensation." This is meant to help with medical bills and mental health counseling that are often the results of domestic violence. But a person can't usually ask for financial help this way unless he or she files a police report.

The "Power and Control Wheel" of Violence

Domestic violence is talked about a lot more these days, but for a person in a violent relationship, it's still all about secrets. It's hard for a person to tell anyone that she's been beaten or that her husband or boyfriend tells her she's a slut or that he's even convinced her she's crazy. It's hard to imagine that anyone would believe her; after all, her husband or boyfriend is so nice to everyone else.

The behavior of abusers does actually follow a pattern, though, and people who work with victims of domestic violence see these patterns a lot. So people who help victims have designed a good way to show those victims how this abusive pattern works. There's a diagram, designed like a wheel and often called the "Power and Control Wheel," because with abusers it's all about keeping the power and the control over the other person.

RESOURCES

You can learn more about the ideas behind this wheel by visiting www.theduluthmodel.org. It's the home page of the Domestic Abuse Intervention Project in Duluth, Minnesota. Click "wheel gallery" to see the diagram. But you can also see the same image by using a search engine on the Web; just type in "power and control wheel." You can also add your state or county to the search terms to learn about organizations in your area that help victims of domestic violence.

Wrongful Accusations of Domestic Violence: Tips for the Accused

Are you thinking that not everyone is honest? You're right. There are some people who decide to make life miserable for their partner during a divorce or breakup. They may claim to be afraid for their life, or claim that they have been the victim of some kind of violence. This type of false claim can cause all sorts of problems for the person who is accused. It's often hard for the court to know who is lying in a case like this.

If you are wrongly accused of domestic violence—and this happens often—it is important to seek legal counsel immediately. Having an **order of protection** entered

TAKE NOTE

against you is serious business. It shows up on your record and can make it difficult for you to get some jobs. If you didn't do what you are accused of, you need to find an experienced lawyer and fight back through the legal system. It is important to gather evidence that supports your innocence, and a good lawyer can help.

What Do You Think?

- There's something in the news about domestic violence every day. Why do you think it's become a common problem? Or do you think maybe it was always a problem, but now more people talk about it?

- Can the police or sheriff guarantee complete protection once a protection order has been entered? Why not?

- Do you know someone who has a big problem with his or her temper? How does this affect that person at work? Try picturing what life is like for this person and his or her family at home.

- Explain to someone else when a problem might be both a family law issue and a criminal issue. Think of a few examples to make it clear.

- If a child sees one parent hit the other parent, what problems could that child have later on?

- Maybe your best friend or your sister keeps going back to the boyfriend (or girlfriend) who abuses her. What can you tell her to help her make better decision?

10 Living Together but Not Married? Nonmarital Relationships

STATUTE

Okay. You're not married and you have no plans to get married. But you and your partner are thinking about moving in together. Or maybe you're already living together. Maybe you've been living together a long time, with kids and all the details of a marriage except the signed paper. Does that mean the rules about marriage and divorce don't apply to you? It depends on what state you live in.

In many states most of the rules that govern the division of property in a divorce also apply to couples who aren't married. And in some cases these rules can apply to same-sex couples who have been living together. Recently some states have enacted specific laws called **"domestic partnership** statues." Let's take a look at a few things to consider in a nonmarital relationship. When you're finished with this chapter, even if you're not married, it's a good idea to give the section on marriage in chapter 4 a careful look.

What about Property?

In most states people who are living together do not necessarily have rights to property owned by one party in his or her separate name. So if the relationship ends, the person who does not own the property may not have any right to it. There is one exception: if the parties share in the expenses and intended to own the property together, the court may decide that the person not on the title has some kind of ownership right. You can see how hard it could be hard to prove this, and that often becomes a problem when a couple decides to split up. Other states with domestic partnership laws specify how property is distributed in a breakup.

TAKE NOTE

The best thing to do, if people are living together, is to put both names on property they purchase. They should also enter into an agreement about the ownership. People typically own property together as joint tenants (fifty-fifty) or tenants in common (meaning that they personally decide the percentage of ownership). If you draw up a legal agreement, you can have it be any way you want; the important thing is to get something legally binding in writing. This is another area where different states have different rules, so getting a lawyer may be absolutely necessary.

Some states consider that a couple who has been together for a long time should be treated as though they are married if it comes to a breakup. This is usually called a **"meretricious relationship."** One reason some states recognize these arrangements is because the couple has shown all the commitments of marriage. Some of these states even allow same-sex couples to claim meretricious relationships and get many of the benefits that married couples do if it comes to property division at the time of breaking up.

His Name's Not on the Title

TAKE NOTE

Here's another small but important detail, and this applies whether you're married or not. Remember in the case study that Insook owned three hair salons. Even if her husband's name wasn't on the title that showed ownership of these businesses, he could still be awarded a part of the value of her property. If you live with someone but aren't married, the court may still give your partner some of your property. It doesn't matter whether his or her name is on the title. The courts decide whether that person has an interest in the property, and it may award some of that property to him or her. States differ as to whether unmarried couples have the right to maintenance or alimony. It's a good idea to check the law in your state if you are living with someone.

And What's a Domestic Partnership?

Some states recognize the concept of "domestic partnership," which is used to describe a couple who lives together without being married. It is a little bit like the modern term for a "common-law relationship," except that in many places a domestic partnership includes gay and lesbian relationships.

There are ways to describe a couple in a domestic partnership. Look at this list below and see if it describes you or anyone you know. This description of domestic partnership comes from Florida; it may not be the same where you live.

- Each party is at least eighteen years old and competent to form a contract.
- Neither party is married nor a partner to another domestic partnership relationship.
- Each party is the other person's only partner.
- Each party is not related to the other by blood.
- Both parties agree to be jointly responsible for each other's basic food, shelter, and the basics of life.
- Each party considers himself/herself to be a member of the immediate family of the other partner.

Possible Benefits of a Domestic Partnership

If you're in a committed relationship but don't have a marriage certificate, there are still some ways you might benefit. But don't take this for granted, because the rules are different from state to state. In some cases the rules are different if the couple is gay or straight. One benefit of registering as domestic partner is that the statutes may direct how finances and property are handled in a breakup.

Social Security benefits for your domestic partner aren't automatic. When a married person dies, the widow or widower can usually get part of that person's Social Security, and minor children might also get Supplemental Income from Social Security. In some families this extra income makes a big difference in their ability to pay the bills each month. But there's no guarantee about this in the case of unmarried or gay couples. The solution: learn how the rules about Social Security benefits affect you before you move in with someone. You could begin by going to this Web site: <u>www.ssa.gov/gethelp1.htm</u>.

RESOURCES

Pensions, Health Insurance, Life Insurance

When a spouse dies, the widow or widower can usually collect part of any pension from that spouse's working years. So if your wife worked for the Transit Authority for thirty years, you probably could collect some of her pension. This is a well-known benefit of being married. Does it work the same way for domestic partnerships? Not so easily. In many cases the authorities who manage pensions can't legally make payments to a surviving spouse without proof of a marriage.

The same is true for health insurance and life insurance. Some cities and counties are trying to change the rules so that a domestic partnership can have the same benefits as a married couple. But this isn't the case all over the country. Let's say your neighbor works for the shipyard and his girlfriend stays at home. It's not automatic that she can get medical coverage. He would have to be very careful too to make sure she is a beneficiary if he buys life insurance, because it's not automatic.

TAKE NOTE

Again, the message is to do your homework. Find out what is legal in your state regarding whatever relationship you're in or thinking about. The best time to do this is before you take that big step and move in together. And it's important to be able to talk to your mate about difficult details, like what would happen if one of you died or if you split up.

All these same concerns make sense if you're talking about any children getting benefits. For example, sometimes a disabled child can get Social Security income through a parent. In these cases it's important to be able to prove that there was a marriage or proof that the adult was the actual parent. Check on the importance of proof of parentage (who the real parent is) in chapter 7. And here's an important point to remember if there are children in an unmarried relationship: the same rules usually apply about relocating children who are subject to a parenting plan properly filed in the court, or changing the court-approved parenting plan after a breakup, whether or not there was a marriage certificate. Look back at chapter 6 for information on your responsibilities as a parent.

What Do You Think?

- Your friend is so excited because her boyfriend asked her to move in with him. What could you suggest she do before she decides?

- Some important court cases involve situations between gay couples who are splitting up. See if you can learn what happened in a recent case like this. Start by looking in your local newspaper or online.

- Everybody has an opinion about whether unmarried or gay couples should have the same rights as married couples. Talk to a friend or coworker and see whether he or she agrees with your views on this topic.

- Find out why a couple you know has chosen not to get married. Or if that describes you, give reasons for your choice.

- Is it legal for insurance policies where you live to cover domestic partners? Find out whether this is the same if the couple is gay or straight.

11 Details, Details: It Doesn't End at the Courthouse

TAKE NOTE

We've talked about the big issues in a divorce or breakup. Those things include dividing up any property or debts. Child custody is a difficult and often painful question. Selling the family home might be a big challenge. With all these big questions, it's easy to overlook other details—some really big ones—that could affect how smoothly your life goes in those first years after a divorce.

Bank Accounts, Pensions, Insurance, Wills

If a couple has both their names on insurance documents, retirement accounts, bank accounts, and so forth, they need to change these accounts when a divorce is final. They need to change names on several different accounts, and most of the time the company that holds the account needs some kind of proof of divorce to make the changes. It is helpful to have extra copies of the divorce decree handy.

The same thing is true for other ownership papers. If the house goes to one person in the divorce, or even the car, make sure any bank or loan papers or titles show only the one name. This usually requires the party who gets the property to refinance it to take the other person's name off of the loan. So when dividing up the assets in a divorce, before you sign the final documents, be sure that the person who gets the house can refinance it. Otherwise it's best to sell the house.

One of the most important things to change is your will. If you have even a simple will, it says who would get your property after your death. You want to make sure your will has the right names on it.

How about your credit cards? Get credit cards in your own name and cancel any cards you held jointly with your ex.

Get new health insurance. This is especially important when one spouse has been covered by the other's plan through his or her workplace. It's a detail that's easy to forget, but unexpected medical bills can really make a mess of a budget. In most cases the spouse can get COBRA insurance for a period of time after the divorce, but COBRA is usually very expensive, so check this out before you make any agreements about who is going to pay the COBRA premiums. COBRA is the term for a temporary health coverage plan passed by Congress in 1986 (the Consolidated Omnibus Budget Reconciliation Act), and it might be helpful in the first few months after a divorce. You can learn more about COBRA and what the letters stand for by visiting the Web site of the U.S. Department of Labor (www.dol.gov). Use the search tool on the home page to get more information.

RESOURCES

CHAPTER 11

I Never Thought of That

Talk to anyone who's recently gotten a divorce, and they could give you a list of all the little details to take care of. Here are just a few examples:

- You may want to change the locks on the house, for a greater sense of security.
- Try to cooperate with your ex to be sure any personal property is out of the house. This is often a touchy subject in a divorce, and compromising on these issues can help to be sure there are no more hard feelings than necessary.
- If you have young children, make sure the school or day care providers know who can legally pick them up from school or day care. Make sure anyone who cares for your kids has up-to-date contact numbers in case of an emergency.
- Noncustodial parents should think about volunteering at school. Get involved in school activities, chaperone on field trips, get to know the teacher, and get your name on the teacher's e-mail list. This helps you stay in your child's life, and you'll be able to keep little problems from getting too big. You could also volunteer to coach or help manage your child's sports team.
- If each of you kept a vehicle as part of the divorce settlement, make sure you transfer the titles so that the correct party's name is on the vehicle he or she now owns.
- Check your credit history when divorce proceedings start and make sure accounts reflect that you are now the only name on your credit account.

What Do You Think?

- If you've been divorced, what do you think was the hardest part?

- Your friend has split from her boyfriend, and their child is in day care a lot. She's worried that her ex may try to take the child from the day care. What could you tell her to do?

- How many other people have keys to your place, besides your spouse or partner?

- Make a list of assets you own that you would have to transfer title to in the event of a divorce.

- Now make a list of loans or debts that would have to be transferred as well.

12 Other Issues

Have we covered everything there is to know about marriage and family law and divorce? Well, not exactly, but you have the basics. The two issues we look at in this chapter are interesting and may affect you or a relative or friend.

Prenuptial Agreements

When we hear about prenuptial agreements, most of us think of famous and wealthy people. Those things are just for the really rich people, right? Not exactly. A prenuptial agreement is an agreement that a couple signs before they get married. Sometimes it's called an **antenuptial agreement**. An agreement like this usually contains a list of all of the parties' assets and who owns what at the time of marriage. Most prenuptial agreements are used by people with assets at the time they marry. "Prenups" typically spell out how the couple will handle financial decisions during marriage. They may also decide how property would be distributed if there is a divorce.

Please note: Prenups are tricky documents. Most states have specific requirements that must be included for a

TAKE NOTE

prenup to be valid. The most important requirement is that the agreement be fair. In most states the spouse with the money and assets can't write a prenup saying the other spouse will get nothing if you later divorce. It's a good idea to talk to a lawyer if you are thinking of a prenup.

Special Rules for Military Families

The law has always tried to protect the servicemen and servicewomen who represent the United States. One law was the Soldiers and Sailors Civil Relief Act of 1918, which was updated just before World War II, in 1940. Our lawmakers in Congress looked at these laws again in 2003. One thing they changed was the name: the 2003 law is now known as the Servicemembers Civil Relief Act.

This act protects both military personnel and members of the National Guard or Reserves. There are many parts to this act, but the main goal is to prevent service members from having to defend themselves in certain kinds of civil actions while they're on active duty. You can imagine how hard it would be for soldiers or sailors to concentrate on their dangerous job if they're worried about whether their family is about to be thrown out of the house because they can't make the rent.

STATUTE

What does this have to do with divorce? Let's say a wife files for divorce while her husband is deployed, on active duty and away from home. If the husband requests a "stay" of the proceedings, the courts cannot act on that request for a divorce. They have to wait until the spouse is able to participate in the process, and that could take many months or longer. What if that spouse decided not to send support to his wife and kids, because he was

TAKE NOTE

unhappy that she wanted a divorce? The court may not be able to order temporary support, so the family would get a small amount of income from the military to live on while they waited for the servicemember to return from duty.

Here's a perfect example of why you should look into your situation carefully before you take steps toward a divorce: Maybe your wife is a nurse in the Army Reserve. She's working stateside for the local hospital, and you decide to get a divorce. Then she gets called up for active duty. The courts may not be able to make any rulings in the case until she is able to return and take part in the process.

If you see a lawyer about a possible divorce, be sure to talk with her or him about whether your spouse is in any branch of military service, even if he or she is not currently active. It's the only way to protect yourself and your kids.

 ## What Do You Think?

- Take the side of the sailor or soldier in a divorce proceeding. Explain why he or she shouldn't be expected to deal with a divorce when on active duty.
- Do you know anyone who signed a prenuptial agreement? What were their reasons?
- Why do you think there is a law especially for members of the armed services? Why does it only apply to those on active duty?
- Let's say your uncle is widowed; he has a business

and three grown children. He's thinking about getting married again and you want him to consider a pre-nuptial agreement. How could you encourage him to do this without saying unkind or unfair things about his girlfriend?

Summary of Statutes

Consolidated Omnibus Budget Reconciliation Act of 1986

The Hague Convention (1996)

Nineteenth Amendment of the United States Constitution (1919)

Servicemembers Civil Relief Act of 2003

Soldiers and Sailors Civil Relief Act of 1918

Uniform Child Custody Jurisdiction and Enforcement Act of 1997

Six Things to Consider If You Think Your Marriage Is Ending

There's so much to think about, it may seem impossible to remember everything you've read about in this *Your Rights in Divorce and Child Custody: Legal Guide*. The best part is that you can refer back to it again and again. If you have reason to think your marriage or relationship might be in trouble, or if a friend or family member has asked your advice, you'll find good ideas in this guide on how to protect yourself or your friend.

But in the meantime, here is a short list of the six most important things to remember about marriage and family law. Look over these six pointers; they'll help you in a variety of ways. They'll suggest things that can help you with the financial problems that often go with divorce. There are practical steps as well that deal with custody questions. And most of all, following these six things might mean a more stable life after a divorce or breakup.

 If You Think Your Marriage Might Be Ending

1. Do your homework about the laws in your state.
2. Keep all important official documents, or copies of documents, in a safe place.
3. Be sure you know about all of your finances.

4. Establish some financial accounts in your own name.

5. Keep your emotions under control.

6. Recognize that stability for the kids must take priority over your personal needs during the divorce process and after.

1. **Do your homework about the laws in your state.** Learn about custody rules before you walk out and leave the kids with your spouse. Find out whether there is some kind of waiting period before you can be divorced. Learn what your state says about marital property *before* you take steps that might make it hard to divide shared property in a fair way. Find out if you live in a fault or no-fault state.

2. **Keep all important official documents, or copies of documents, in a safe place.** If you or your kids have a passport, keep it locked up. The same is true for wills, insurance policies, car registrations, records of retirement accounts, or proof of property ownership. Make sure you have the account numbers for all bank and investment accounts.

3. **Be sure you know about all of your finances.** If you believe you are headed for divorce, the best thing to do is make copies of all of your financial statements and debts. Look around the house for any unfamiliar accounts, like credit cards or bank accounts, that you didn't know about. Make copies of those statements or at least write down the account numbers. Educate yourself, especially if your spouse has handled all the financial matters.

4. **Establish some financial accounts in your own name.** If the spouse in #3 could be you, make some changes. Start a bank account with only your name on it, and apply for a credit card with only your name, but be sure not to run up a lot of charges on it. What you'll be doing is establishing a safe credit history that could help a lot if you're suddenly on your own. Use a P.O. box or a friend's address if you are concerned that your spouse could find out about the account.

5. **Keep your emotions under control.** There isn't a single part of the divorce process that is easy, and most steps stir up strong emotions. You might get very angry, sad, discouraged, or depressed. You'll need to get all these emotions under control to reach an agreement with your ex about how to split assets and how to arrange custody of minor children. Talk to a friend, seek counseling, or find a support group, but don't let those emotions control you.

6. **Recognize that stability for the kids must take priority over your personal needs during the divorce process and after.** Remind yourself that the divorce is not the kids' fault—they got caught in the middle. Do everything you can to keep their lives as stable as possible. This will help them, but it will also help you in setting up a reasonable custody or parenting plan and also in maintaining a civil relationship with your ex after the divorce process is completed. And never move out of your house without understanding your rights.

Glossary

Note: The following definitions are explained in terms of the law. These terms may have slightly different meanings when used in other ways.

affidavit. A signed legal document that is a declared statement of facts signed under penalty of perjury.

alimony. Also called "maintenance," this is the requirement that one divorcing spouse provide some kind of court-assigned financial support to the other spouse.

alternative dispute resolution. Also known as ADR, this is the process, including mediation and arbitration, of settling a dispute without going to court.

antenuptial agreement. An agreement made before getting married that identifies which property is separate and how property will be distributed in case of divorce; also called a "prenuptial agreement."

arbitration. The process of settling a disagreement by having a neutral third party listen to both sides. That person then makes a decision about how to settle the disagreement. Both sides have to obey this decision.

assets. Property of meaningful value, such as a car, a home, real estate, money, and investments, including retirement accounts.

child custody. This concerns the question of who is responsible for the day-to-day care of minor children after a family splits up.

child custody plan. A plan that states the schedule for where the children will live and how they will be cared for after a divorce. Also called a "parenting plan."

common-law relationship. Some states use this name to describe the legal relationship between a couple when they've lived together for a long time but never got married. They're also called "meretricious relationships." Different states have different laws about these relationships.

community property state. The term used in the states where a married couple owns equally all of the assets they acquired during the course of their marriage.

contract. A legal agreement in which the parties exchange a promise.

custodial interference. When one parent interferes with the rights of the other parent, usually by moving or traveling with the child without the permission of the other parent.

custody arrangement. The plan that states the schedule for the children after a divorce. Also called a "child custody plan" or a "parenting plan."

defendant. The party sued in a civil lawsuit or the party charged with a crime in a criminal prosecution. In some of types of cases, such as divorce, a defendant may be called a "respondent." (see: plaintiff)

deposition. Sworn testimony given under oath in the presence of a court reporter who transcribes everything that is said.

discovery. The legal process used in a lawsuit by which the requesting party obtains information about the other party. In divorces, this usually involves learning information about finances, records, debts, and so on of the other party. This is usually done through written questions, sworn testimony, or subpoenas.

dissolution of marriage. The official term for when the court decides that a marriage is dissolved, or over. This is another term for divorce.

domestic partnership. The arrangement when two people live together with the commitments of marriage but without a marriage certificate. Some states have specifics laws that define domestic partnerships.

equitable distribution. The idea that assets are divided in a fair manner in a divorce.

grounds for divorce. These refer to the specific reasons for why a divorce is being requested. Not all states require a reason for a person to request a divorce.

guardian *ad litem*. A court-appointed person who speaks on behalf of a minor child.

intangible asset. Property that has value but that can't be easily measured, such as a medical degree or a business that has earning power or value.

interrogatories. A series of written questions one party can send to the other party in order to gain information. The questions must be answered truthfully, within a certain period of time, and must be signed under penalty of perjury.

irreconcilable differences. In family law, this refers to when a married couple seeks a divorce with the reason given that they can't get along.

joint custody. When both parents share in the care and decision-making for their minor children after a divorce.

jurisdiction. When a lawsuit is filed, such as a divorce, the court has the authority to make decisions about the parties. Any requests the parties have can be presented to the court in the form of a motion. The court hears the motion and makes a decision called an "order." The parties must follow the court order or be faced with contempt of court.

legal separation. This is a term that has very different meanings in different states. In some states it's the period of time while waiting for a divorce to be final. In other states it's like a divorce; the parties distribute their assets and enter a custody arrangement, but they can continue some of the benefits of marriage, such as staying on the other person's health insurance.

lien. When one party owes another party money, the person who is owed the money takes an interest in the other person's property. Their interest lasts until they get paid back. To be sure this happens, they file a legal document, called a lien, on the person's property.

maintenance. Also called "alimony," this is the requirement that one divorcing spouse provide some kind of court-assigned financial support to the other spouse.

mediation. The process of resolving a dispute with the assistance of a neutral third party who facilitates the settlement process.

meretricious relationship. This term describes the legal relationship between a couple when they've lived together but never got married, similar to common-law relationships. Different states have different laws about these marriage-like relationships.

neutral exchange site. A place where kids can be dropped off or picked up by parents who can't deal with each other, so the kids are safe and there are less likely to be fights or arguments between the parents. The neutral exchange site is usually a public place where there are lots of people around.

no-fault divorce. The policy of many states that says a divorcing couple doesn't have to give reasons for their divorce.

order of protection. Also called a "protection order" or a "restraining order" this is a court order to a person to avoid contact with the person who is protected under the order. The person who wants to be protected by this kind of order has to prove that he or she is afraid for his or her safety. If the order is violated, the person violating the order may have to go to jail.

parenting classes. These classes, offered in most communities, teach adults how to talk to, listen to, and play with their kids in a healthy way.

parenting evaluator. A trained person who observes parents and children together, asks questions, and talks to people who know the family, so he or she can report an opinion to the court about the best parenting or custody plan for the children after a divorce.

parenting history survey. One of the tools used by a parenting evaluator to see what kind of parenting skills a person has.

parenting plan. A plan that states the schedule for the children after a divorce. Also called a "child custody plan" or a "custody arrangement."

petition. The formal document that starts a divorce proceeding or asks the court to enter an order for protection.

petitioner. The party who presents a formal written petition to the court. In a lawsuit this party is called the "plaintiff."

plaintiff. The party who sues another by filing a complaint with the court against the defendant(s). (*See also* **complaint, defendant, petitioner**)

prenuptial agreement. This is the same as an antenuptial agreement.

protection order. Also called an "order of protection," this is a court order to a person to avoid contact with the person who is protected under the order. If the order is violated, the person violating the order can go to jail.

primary residential parent. Another term for the parent who has the children most of the time after divorce.

respondent. The party who must answer a petition requiring a rspondent to take some kind of action. In such cases the person filing the petition is called the "petitioner." In a lawsuit, the respondent is called the "defendant."

restraining orders. These court orders instruct one party to stay away from another party, usually the other spouse or children. In the case of financial restraining orders, the orders instruct the parties during the divorce process not to spend money other than what they need to get by, not to sell anything, or move any bank accounts, cancel any insurance policies, or change any wills, and so on.

separate property. The term used mostly in community-property states to define property that was either owned before marriage, received as a gift before or during the marriage, or inherited. This property is usually not divided during a divorce.

service of process. When a lawsuit, such as a divorce, is filed, it must be served on the other party by having a person who is not one of the parties to the lawsuit give the court papers to the other party. The person who gives the papers must sign a sworn statement that he or she gave the other party the papers. Once this is filed and served, the lawsuit is officially begun.

subpoena. A formal legal paper that says a person or a representative of a business or institution must testify or in some way supply the information requested in the subpoena.

suffrage. The right to vote.

supervised visits. This refers to cases when a parent must meet with his or her children only when another neutral, trained adult is also present.

temporary orders. These are orders from the court saying who has child custody and who is responsible for what bills and so on before a divorce is final.

third-party custody. The unusual situation when someone other than a parent, such as a grandparent, has custody of minor children.

visitation rights. The rights of a noncustodial parent to have regular contact with his or her children.

Resources

American Bar Association
(child custody issues) www.abanet.org/publiced/
practical/books/family/chapter_12.pdf

American Psychological Association
("Diversity Among Lesbian Mothers, Gay Fathers,
and Their Children")
www.apa.org/pi/lgbc/publications/lgpdiversity.html

Big Brothers Big Sisters
www.bbbs.org

Family Law Organization
www.familylaw.org/familylawcode.htm

FindLaw: State Laws on Divorce and Child Custody
http://family.findlaw.com/divorce/state-divorce-laws

State Bar of Georgia
(divorce information)
www.gabar.org/communications/consumer_pamphlet_
series/divorce

LawHelp.org
(information on family law, divorce in various parts of
the United States)
www.lawhelp.org

Law Library of Congress
(Married Women's Property Law)
http://memory.loc.gov/ammem/awhhtml/awlaw3/
property_law.html

Legal Aid of South Florida
www.legalaid.org

Legal Information Institute of Cornell Law School
www.law.cornell.edu/wex/state_statutes

Minnesota Program Development, Inc.
(Duluth, Minnesota, Domestic Abuse Intervention Project)
www.theduluthmodel.org

National Domestic Violence Hotline
www.ndvh.org

Northwest Women's Law Center
("Information for Parents in Treatment on: Dependency
and Custody Actions")
www.nwwlc.org/publications/family/
CustodyDependency02.pdf

Official California Legislative Information
www.leginfo.ca.gov/calaw.html

Parents without Partners
www.parentswithoutpartners.org

Social Security Administration
("Marriage, Divorce, and Name Changes")
www.ssa.gov/gethelp1.htm

Southern Poverty Law Center
www.splcenter.org/center/about.jsp

United States Department of Justice
www.usdoj.gov

University of Pennsylvania
("Uniform Child Custody Jurisdiction Act")
www.law.upenn.edu/bll/ulc/fnact99/1920 69/
uccja68.htm

Washington State Bar Association
"(Dissolution of Marriage (Divorce)"
www.wsba.org/media/publications/pamphlets/
dissolution.htm

Since the hyperlinks listed here may change, if you encounter a broken link, please type the name of the organization you wish to look up into your Internet search engine. The name and web address of the organization will probably appear in your search results, and you can follow the new link to the web site.

For a more complete list of resources, go to www.CivilSurvival.com.

Index

A

abuse. *See* domestic violence
abuse, emotional, 58
ADR. *See* alternative dispute resolution
affidavit, 75, 124
age of children, 58
age of spouses, 44, 58, 80
alimony, 46, 79–83, 124
alternative dispute resolution, 96, 124
American Bar Association, 131
American Psychological Association, 131
anger management, 100
antenuptial agreement, 124.
  See also prenuptial agreement
arbitration, 88, 124
assets, 29, 45–48, 124
attorneys, choosing, 6–10, 14–18, 88–89

B

bank accounts, 112–113
"best interests of the children"
  case study, 6–8, 11–13
  child protective services intervention, 59
  nonpayment of child support, 76
  overview, 51–53
  patience, 97
  preparing for divorce, 121–123
  relocation, 64
  third-party custody, 67
Big Brothers Big Sisters, 131
birth certificate, 75
business ownership, 46–47

C

California Legislative Information, 86, 132

car loans, 35, 48, 112–113
career enhancement, 46, 80–81.
  See also employability of spouses
case study, 5–21
changing the locks, 114
changing your name, 132
child care notification, 114
child custody, 124, 131. *See also* under custodial, custody
child custody plan
  definition, 125
  overview, 55
  some questions to consider, 52, 57–59
  See also custody arrangement; parenting plan
child protective services intervention, 59, 66–67
child support, 72–77, 80
children's benefits in a domestic partnership, 110–111
children's issues, considered in hiring an attorney, 88
children's reactions to divorce, 5–6, 20–21, 67–70
children's wishes, considered in the parenting plan, 57
choosing an attorney, 6–10, 14–18, 88–89
COBRA, 113
commingled assets, 30–31, 34
common-law relationship, 108–109, 125
community property, 32–34
community property states, 32, 125
compensation for crime victims, 103
Consolidated Omnibus Budget Reconciliation Act of 1986, 113, 120
contempt of court. *See* jurisdiction
contract, 28–29, 125

control wheel of domestic
    violence, 103–104
Cornell Law School, Legal
    Information Institute, 132
court orders. *See* financial
    restraining order; jurisdiction;
    order of protection;
    protection order; restraining
    order; temporary orders
CPS. *See* child protective services
    intervention
credit card accounts, 113
credit card debt, 35, 48–49
credit history, 114
crime victim compensation, 103
criminal activity and custody,
    66–67
cultural issues, considered in the
    parenting plan, 57
custodial interference, 64, 125
custodial parent, 53
custody
    arrangement overview, 55–56
    "best interests of the
        children," 51–52
    international issues, 64–66
    interstate issues, 62, 63–64
    joint custody, 54, 126
    jurisdiction, 52–53
    modifications to, between
        states, 62
    parental disagreement, 59–61
    questions to consider, 57–59
    relocation, 63–66
    statutes overview, 53–54
    substance abuse issues and,
        132
    support payments and, 73
    types of, 54–55
custody arrangement. *See*
    also child custody plan;
    parenting plan
    definition, 125
    jurisdiction and, 39–41
    overview, 55–56
    temporary orders, 94

D

day care notification, 114
deadbeat parents, 76
debts, 35, 48–49
decision making about the kids, 56
decree of divorce, 97–98
defendant, 91, 100, 125
dependency. *See under* substance
    abuse issues
deposition, 95, 125
discipline style, considered in the
    parenting plan, 58
discovery, 94–95, 125–126
dissolution of marriage, 90, 126. *See
    also* divorce
divorce
    alternative dispute resolution, 96
    choosing an attorney, 88–89
    discovery, 94–95
    filing, 90–91
    final decree, 97–98
    learning about your state laws,
        86–87
    preparing for, 121–123
    representing yourself, or not, 86–89
    resources, 131–133
    temporary orders, 91–94
    time required, 96–97
    See also dissolution of
        marriage
divorce, no-fault, 128
Domestic Abuse Intervention
    Project, 104, 132
domestic partnership, 106–111, 126
domestic partnership and child
    support, 74–76
domestic violence, 99–105
    advocates for victims, 100
    considered in the parenting plan, 58
    custody issues and, 56, 62–63
    Domestic Abuse Intervention
        Project, 104, 132
    resources, 132
    suffrage and, 25
    tips for victims, 102–104
Duluth Model of domestic violence,
    104

E

educational expenses and child support, 74
emergency parenting plan, 100
emotional abuse, considered in the parenting plan, 58
employability of spouses, 44, 80. *See also* career enhancement
equitable distribution
    assets and debts, overview, 43–50
    definition, 126
    women's property law and, 24
expense, considered in hiring an attorney, 88
extended family, considered in the parenting plan, 58

F

family, various forms of, 26
Family Law Organization, 131
father, identified on the birth certificate, 75
fault, 44. *See also* no-fault
fault-only states, 37. *See* also no-fault states
fifty-fifty vs. in common ownership, 107
filing for divorce, 90–91
financial information, 93
financial restraining order, 129
financial situation of spouses, considered in alimony, 80
FindLaw: State Laws on Divorce and Child Custody, 131
firearms, 100
Florida Legal Aid (South Florida), 132
future expenses and child support, 74

G

garnishment of wages, 76
gay and lesbian domestic partnership status, 109
gay and lesbian parents, 131
Georgia State Bar Association, 131

gifts as property, 34
going to court, or not, 86–88
good will as an intangible asset, 46–47
grandparents' rights, 67
grounds for divorce, 37–38, 126
guardian *ad litem,* 59, 70, 126

H

Hague Convention, The (1996), 65, 120
health insurance benefits, 110, 112–113
health of spouses, 44, 80
hiring an attorney, or not, 88–89
home state of the children, 61–62

I

in common vs. fifty-fifty ownership, 107
income, past, present, and future, 44, 80–81
inheritance as separate property, 34
intangible assets, 29, 45–48, 126
international custody issues, 64–66
interrogatories, 95, 126
interstate custody issues, 62, 63–64
investment accounts, 112–113
irreconcilable differences, 38, 126

J

joint custody, 54, 126
jurisdiction
    in alimony decisions, 79–80
    child custody and, 52–53
    conferred when filing, 90–91
    considered in the parenting plan, 58
    definition, 127
    during discovery, 95
    overview, 39–41

K

Key Points icon, 4
kidnapping, 62–63, 64

L

Law Library of Congress, 132